GARDEN TOURS OF ENGLAND

Self Guided Tours of

LONDON to THE LAKE DISTRICT

Bonnie Randall

Photographs and Illustrations by
Greg Randall

Windsor Hill Publishing

Illustrations, Maps & Photographs: Greg Randall
Cover Design: Greg Randall & Bonnie Randall

Copyright 1999 by Bonnie Randall's Garden Tours of England. All Rights Reserved.
This book or parts thereof may not be reproduced in any form without obtaining written permission from the publisher: Windsor Hill Publishing, 119 Poppy Court, Walnut Creek, California 94596, tel: (925) 934-7761

Distributed U.S.A.: Windsor Hill Publishing

Randall, Bonnie, 1949-
Garden Tours of England- London to The Lake District
1. Garden Tour- England, 2. Guidebooks, 3. London, 4. Lake District, 5. Yorkshire, 6.Derbyshire

ISBN-0-965651029

Library of Congress Catalog Card Number: 98-92338

Cover Photo: Newby Hall, Yorkshire

To
Rosemary Verey, Penelope Hobhouse,
Christopher Lloyd and All the Other
Designers and Plantsmen
Present and Past
who have given us such wonderful
English gardens

The charm of of stone buildings and walls
can be found all over the Lake District.

• TABLE OF CONTENTS •

		Page
Introduction		ix
Helpful Hints		5
Lake District		11
Tours from London to the Lake District		
Tour 1	Hampton Court, Claremont Landscape Garden, Wisley Garden Daily	18
Tour 2	Clivenden, Englefield House, Savill/Valley Gardens Monday through Thursday	22
Tour 3	Hatfield House, Knebworth House, Myddelton House, St. Albans Monday through Friday	26
Tour 4	Swiss Garden, Wrest Park Garden, St. Albans Saturday & Sunday	30
Tour 5	Castle Ashby, Coton Manor Garden, Holdenby House Wednesday, Thursday, Friday, Sunday	34
Tour 6	Canons Ashby House, Sulgrave Manor, Stowe Landscape Saturday through Tuesday	38
Tour 7	Melbourne Hall, Kedleston Hall, Newstead Abbey Saturday, Sunday, Wednesday	42
Tour 8	Haddon Hall, Chatsworth, Renishaw Hall Friday, Saturday, Sunday	46
Tour 9	Newstead Abbey, Hardwick Hall, Renishaw Hall Friday, Saturday, Sunday	50
Tour 10	Hardwick Hall, Haddon Hall, Chatsworth Monday through Thursday	54
Tour 11	Holker Hall, Levens Hall, Sizergh Castle Sunday through Thursday	58
Tour 12	Hutton-in-the-Forest, Dalemain, Acorn Bank Garden Daily except Friday & Saturday	62
Tour 13	Holehird, Brantwood, Rydal Mount Daily	66
Tour 14	Parcevall Hall Garden, Studley Royal/Fountains Abbey, Newby Hall Daily except Monday	70
Tour 15	Harlow Carr Botanical Garden, Harewood House, Lotherton Hall Daily	74
Tour 16	Beningbrough Hall, Newby Hall, Harlow Carr Botanical Garden Saturday, Sunday, Tuesday, Wednesday	78
Tour 17	Kensinton Gardens, Kew, Chelsea Physic Garden, Fenton House Wednesday through Sunday	82
Garden Descriptions		89
Biographies of Gardeners		101
Garden Design Periods		113
Glossary of Terms		121
Garden Particulars		125
List of Publications		129
Index		131
Order Forms		137

Enjoy colorful pots of flowers,
as the English do, everywhere.

• INTRODUCTION •

Welcome to my third book. Now that I have spent the last three years traveling in England and visiting over 160 gardens in preparation for writing the books, I'm even more convinced that I had a great idea. Afterall, my husband and I are experienced travelers and it still took several guide books, garden books, maps, an atlas and many hours to map out each trip.

My idea, you see, and the goal of each book, is to provide a travel guide that will eliminate most of the confusion and complications travelers run into when planning a trip to the fabulous gardens of England. In this book you will have the information and directions you need to really enjoy your trip. Remember, unlike in the U.S., every garden is not open daily from 9:00 to 5:00. Infact, some gardens are only open one day a week and some are only open between 2:00 and 6:00 in the afternoon. Directional signs are, let's face it, different and not always terribly clear. Then there are those roundabouts and you have to drive on the left hand side of the road. Well, believe me, you'll get used to it and it is all worth it.

This third book takes you from London to the Lake District and includes York and the Peak District. This is a large territory and very diverse in climate, topography, architecture and garden style. You will find quaint villages, large country estates, countryside dotted with sheep and cattle, miles of stone walls, sparkling lakes and beautiful moors and mountains. More importantly, you will find some of the most famous gardens in Europe and several other gardens that, although not nearly as famous, are just as wonderful.

This book describes 17 tours. They are organized by day of the week, with the intention that you will not have to drive far between gardens or feel the need to rush from one to the other. First, determine the day (or days) of the week that you have available. Then find the tours that are open on those days and finally, select the specific tour (s) you are interested in. Brief descriptions and histories of each garden are provided to help you make your selection. Under "List of Publications" you will find several suggestions for colorful picture books that focus on this region and there are many more to choose from in your local book stores. Purchase one or two and get a glimpse of the wondrous gardens that await you.

There are many kinds of gardens in these tours. Some are beautiful flower gardens with herbaceous borders and climbing roses. Some are very formal with large fountains and glorious sculptures and for some, the beauty is found in the history and architecture. For all of the gardens, the enjoyment is in the whole; the design, the history, the house (castle or manor), the countryside and the garden. Take time to experience it all!

No time to waste! There's a lot to see so lets get started!

GARDEN TOURS
OF
ENGLAND

LONDON to
THE LAKE DISTRICT

ENGLAND
MAP

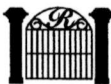

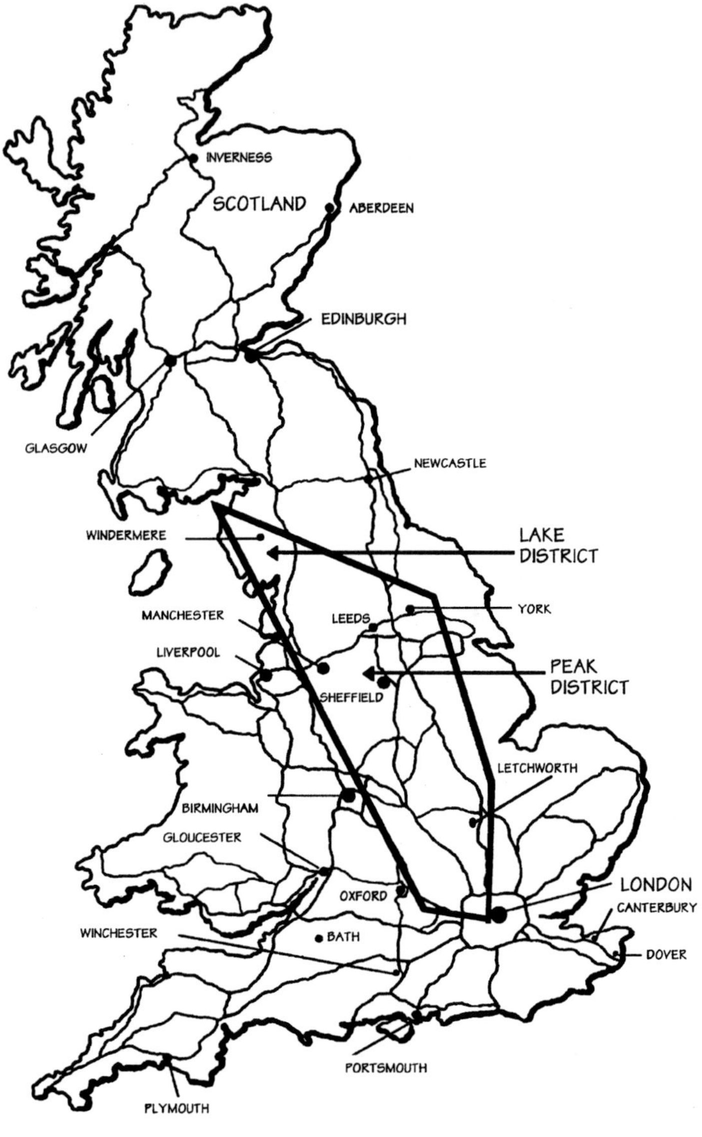
INVERNESS
SCOTLAND
ABERDEEN
EDINBURGH
GLASGOW
NEWCASTLE
WINDERMERE
LAKE
DISTRICT
MANCHESTER
LEEDS
YORK
LIVERPOOL
PEAK
DISTRICT
SHEFFIELD
LETCHWORTH
BIRMINGHAM
GLOUCESTER
OXFORD
LONDON
CANTERBURY
WINCHESTER
BATH
DOVER
PORTSMOUTH
PLYMOUTH

LONDON to THE LAKE DISTRICT
MAP

Harewood House

• HELPFUL HINTS •

• The maps you will find in this book are useful. They are drawn to scale and you should have no trouble following them but, an atlas or road map of England is a must! There are numerous country roads and if you take a wrong turn, you can get confused and lost very quickly. Maps are available at book and travel stores and you should pick one up before you leave.

• Wear comfortable shoes. You will be doing a lot of walking and most of the time it's on dirt or gravel and up and down stairs.

• Wear comfortable clothes. In the summer you may be able to dress light but always bring along a sweater or sweatshirt and possibly a lightweight jacket. Warmer clothes will probably be needed in the spring and fall. A rain coat or slicker is good too.

• Make sure an umbrella is available all year round. We've been very lucky in all our trips but that doesn't mean you will be.

• Bring lots of film. Although there is film and disposable cameras everywhere, it's never around when you really want it and it's usually more expensive.

• Keep your eyes and ears open, many private homes open-up their gardens to the public one or two afternoons a year. If you are lucky, you might have the opportunity to visit a few. Look for signs along the road or in the towns and villages you are visiting. Also, *The Yellow Book* on the "List of Publications" can be ordered and will provide a lot more information on local gardens.

• This area is chock full of charming inns and B&B's; Monkey Island Hotel near Bray-on-Thames, Cliveden near Maidenhead, Redcoats Farmhouse Hotel near Hitchin, New Bath Hotel in Matlock, Graythwaite Manor in Grange-over-Sands, Langdale Chase Hotel in Winderemere, The Balmoral Hotel in Harrogate are but a few. See "List of Publications" for further information or contact your travel agent.

Hints (continued):

- Many of the gardens have food services for lunch and/or tea. Usually nothing extravagant but frequently tasty (some of the pastries at tea are great). There is also hearty fare at most of the pubs and there are little restaurants in many towns and villages.

- I recommend you join the National Trust if you plan on visiting three or more National Trust gardens during your visit (two people, six total admissions). See page 8 for more information on the National Trust.

- The guide books and maps you find at many of the gardens are invaluable and are usually worth the few pounds. The National Trust books are especially good.

- Many of the gardens in this book are open on days other than those listed in the tours. See Garden Particulars on pages 125 thru 127 for further information.

- There are several gardens listed in Garden Particulars (pages 125 thru 127) and Garden Descriptions (pages 89 thru 100) that are not included in the tours. These are not quite up to my standards but that doesn't mean they aren't worth a visit if you are in the area.

- The months, days and times of operation were confirmed prior to publication of this book. Keep in mind that changes may be made to these schedules. It is advisable to confirm the times prior to setting out on your day's tour.

- We found even more interesting garden benches on this trip so we extended our picture collection. You will find several of these throughout this book. Hope you enjoy!

Once again I had to marvel at the beautifully planted, colorful pots that are everywhere. They just have a way of putting it all together that 'we' just can't quite achieve.

- Oh, by the way, listen to Ken Bruce on BBC2 as you are driving around on week day mornings. A little music, a little humor and a taste of the people and the country.

Transportation

There are several types of transportation available. The simplest is to rent a car and drive yourself. You will be driving on the left side on very narrow roads but it won't take long to adjust. Mid sized cars are the best and ask for an automatic unless you are experienced with a stick. Autos can be rented at the airports and in many of the larger cities. Check with your travel agent or your favorite rental company for locations and availability before you leave on your trip. Remember, our maps are helpful but you really do need an atlas or a good road map of England.

You can also rent a car with driver. This is a relaxing way to travel especially if you just want to take a couple day trips. Although, in many cases, the cars are sedans not limos, they are very comfortable and you can just sit back and enjoy the countryside. If you are as lucky as we were on a couple of occasions, your driver will be a retired major or history professor with some wonderful stories about the towns and taverns you see. You can let your finger do the walking or you can ask at your hotel. This is a common practice and should be readily available even in some of the smaller towns.

Trains can be fun. If you are staying in London and want to spend a few days in the country, you can take a train to a central location such as York or Windermere and rent a car or a car and driver there. The trains in Britain are great! They are clean, safe and on schedule. First class is worth the few extra pounds. Information on passes and schedules are available through your travel agent or the British Tourist Board.

If you are planning a trip to Paris, the Eurostar train through the Chunnel is a terrific way to go. Reservations are necessary. You can make arrangements through your travel agent before you leave on your trip or you can call (0345 30 30 30) anytime during your trip.

THE NATIONAL TRUST

The National Trust, a registered charity, was set up in 1895 to promote "the permanent preservation, for the benefit of the nation, of lands and tenements (including buildings) of beauty or historic interest". The Trust currently cares for almost 600,000 acres of outstanding countryside, 555 miles of unspoiled coastline and has more than 300 historic houses and gardens open to the public.

The Trust is able to declare its property "inalienable" by an Act of Parliament in 1907. This means that once land and buildings are in the Trust's ownership, they can never be sold or mortgaged (although they can be leased). Ownership by the Trust guarantees protection for generations to come.

Memberships in the National Trust provides 45% of the annual income needed by the Trust to look after its properties. Members are given free admission to houses and gardens in its care in recognition of the support members give the Trust.

Americans can also join The Royal Oak Foundation which is the U.S. membership affiliate of the National Trust. The Royal Oak foundation actively supports the Trust's mission and promotes cultural exchanges through scholarships and internships.

Your yearly membership allows free admission to all N.T. properties, a discount on some merchandise and a year of N.T. publications. Keep in mind that Sir Paul McCartney's family home is now a Trust property.

I have also enjoyed a series of lectures sponsored by the Royal Oak Foundation right here in San Francisco. These lectures might also be available in a city near you. Its all a part of your membership.

Ask about becoming a member at any National Trust garden or contact the Royal Oak Foundation at 285 West Broadway, Suite 400, New York, N.Y. 10013-2299, (212) 966-6565, fax (212) 966-6619.

Garden Tours of England

Coton Manor

Hampton Court

Hardwick Hall

• THE LAKE DISTRICT •

Visiting the Lake District is visiting a different kind of England. It is wetter and cooler and although there are several lovely gardens, you will find that the plant material reflects a more woodland setting. It is an area only 30 miles long and 20 miles wide with forests, soft green hills, hundreds of miles of stone walls, winding mountain passes and great panoramas of sparkling blue lakes.

Driving along the narrow mountain roads you will be amazed at how green the landscape is. Standing out against the green are hundreds of miles of stone walls running up and down and around the contours of the land. Who built all those walls anyway? Many farmhouses you see date from the 17th century. They are built from stone and slate mined in the area and designed with small windows and large porches to protect the occupants from the chilling winds.

The traditional way of life for hill people continues to be sheep farming. Grazing sheep can be seen everywhere and as you drive along the mountain roads you may have to stop for a sheep crossing. Keep an eye open for those energetic sheep dogs, they are amazing.

As you might imagine from the name, there are several picturesque lakes. If the winds are up you can sail or windsurf. Or you can enjoy a cruise on Lake Windermere or a Gondola ride on Coniston Water. Or just relax, maybe pack a picnic lunch and enjoy the beautiful panoramic views.

More visitors come to the Lake District than any other part of England. Visitors come from all over the world to spend time in lakeside towns like Bowness, Windermere and Ambleside. They come to shop and enjoy terrific restaurants or to find a quiet place to hillwalk, mountain climb, cycle or birdwatch.

Windermere Lake Cruises leave from Bowness, Ambleside and Lakeside every hour in the summer. The trip takes about one hour and it will give you many photo opportunities.

The Steam Ship 'Gondola', a part of the National Trust, was commissioned in 1858 and remained in service on the lake until 1937. It became a houseboat and in the winter storms of 1963, it was washed ashore. It was carefully restored and re-entered service in 1980. 'Gondola' leaves from Coniston and is a great way to enjoy the beautiful countryside or to visit John Ruskin's home at Brantwood.

The Lake District is famous for its literary history. William Wordsworth spent much of his life here. You can visit two of his homes at Rydal Mount and Dove Cottage and trace many of the walks he enjoyed with his wife Dorothy. The much loved Peter Rabbit made his home in the Lake country. Beatrix Potter fell in love with the Lake District when she was a young girl and many of her children's stories were written at her home, Hill Top. (see page 108) John Ruskin, writer, art critic and social reformer, lived at Brantwood on the shores of Coniston Water. (see page109) Other writers of note who called this home were John Cunliffe, Arthur Ransome and Hugh Walpole and more modern writers like Melvyn Bragg, Hunter Davies and Donna Baker.

A few of the towns and villages you may encounter in your travels through the Lake District are:

Bowness-on-Windermere is a bustling lakeside town with dramatic views. There are many interesting shops to explore, a wide variety of restaurants and pubs and the opportunity for a boat ride on Windermere Lake. You can also enjoy the Beatrix Potter Exhibition and the Steamboat Museum. Busy, busy spot!

Although Windermere is not right on the lake, you will find a charming Victorian town with lots of opportunities to shop and eat. Several lakefront hotels are located just outside of town. It can be reached by train, on the London-Glasgow Intercity line.

Ambleside is a lively village with craftsmen style slate buildings. Again there are many opportunities to shop at small, sophisticated shops.

Grange-upon-Sands, on the southern coast of the Lake District, was connected to the rail network in 1857. If architecture is of interest, stop by the train station or you might want to visit the seaside park and do a little bird watching. The Graythwaite Manor, a lovely country inn might be a spot to stay for a few days. You will enjoy the garden, an ocean view and maybe 18 holes at a near-by golf course. Ask about their five day 'Garden Visits' packages (015395 32001).

• THE PEAK DISTRICT •

I had the opportunity on this trip to visit my homeland, the Peak District. There are many charming towns and beautiful stately homes here but the spectacular scenery we found driving through the National Park just took my breath away. I wanted to snap a hundred pictures so I could show my friends how wonderful the moorlands are but, guess what, I ended up with '0' pictures. You'll just have to take the drive from Prestbury to Grange-upon-Sands yourself.

The Peak District, referred to as 'a massive English rockery', is 30 miles long and 20 miles at its widest point with some peaks as high as 2000 feet. It begins in Derbyshire and runs north into Yorkshire. The beauty of the countryside is in the turf covered plateaus and heather clad moors.

A few of the towns and villages you may encounter in your travels through the Peak District are:

'The Gateway to the Peak' is Glossop. The town is skirted on three sides by the Peak National Park and offers a wide range of accommodations from camping to luxurious hotels. You might want to visit the outdoor market on Friday and Saturday.

Matlock is a great place to visit for the relaxing baths, charming hotels and a variety of restaurants. Take a tram car half-way to the stars and look down on the rugged cliffs overlooking the river and fabulous views of the countryside.

Interesting little town Prestbury, it is one of the most expensive pieces of real estate in England. Take a count of all the Jags. It is a lovely place to stop for the night before heading north through the Peak District and on to the Lake District.

• YORK, ETC •

The city of York is the center of north central England. It was the 19th century hub of Britain's railway system but its history goes back a lot further than that. The Romans built it as a fortress in 71 AD and eight centuries later the Vikings arrived and gave York its name. It was the Normans who made the city a vital center of government, commerce and religion. When the Tudor age began in 1485 it had already reached its zenith. In the 18th century York became a fashionable resort and again a center of prosperity.

There is much to see in York and, if you can, stay in the area a couple days. Plan on a little walking, the town really isn't that big. Your love for gardens is not wasted here. Window boxes and colorful planters are everywhere and the Museum Garden in the heart of York is a good place to stop and relax. If you like Italian food, the area around York is the place for you.

Places of interest:

The Minster is the largest medieval structure in the United Kingdom. Construction began in 1220 and was finally completed in 1472. I was very impressed and moved by the beauty of this cathedral. The stained glass windows, 128 in all, are particularly impressive. The spires can be seen from almost everywhere in the city.

The medieval walls that encircle the city for about three miles have been carefully restored and maintained. A walk along this wall is a must but it will take you almost two hours. The views of the city are fabulous and in the spring you can find a riot of color from hundreds of daffodils.

The Lord Mayor's residence, a wonderful example of Georgian architecture, was built between 1725 and 1730.

York is not only known for its historical significance but it is also a great place to shop and enjoy a plate of pasta or a couple pints. The outdoor market is open seven days a week and you can find fruits, vegetables, fresh flowers and lots of special items to remind you of your visit. If conventional shopping is more to your liking, there is plenty of that too. For instance, stop by Mulberry Hall for fine china and porcelain such as Wedgewood, Royal Doulton and Herend.

Another lovely city not far from York is Harrogate. A town filled with lavish lawns and abundant flower beds was once famed for its waters. This spa town reached its height in popularity during the 18th and 19th centuries after a physician claimed the waters had healing powers. Today you will find several charming small hotels and a large selection of Italian restaurants.

Other cities and places of interest you will find in your travels from London to The Lake District:

Letchworth in Bedfordshire was the first garden city. Created by the great social reformer, Ebenezer Howard, it was used as a yardstick for planned new towns around the world.

Not far from Letchworth and near The Swiss Garden you might want to stop at the Shuttleworth Collection. This world famous collection of vintage planes and vintage cars and motorcycles is open April - October from 10:00 to 5:00.

The charming town of Sulgrave near Sulgrave Manor in Northamptonshire reminds me of the Cotswolds with stone buildings, thatched roofs, flower boxes and small colorful gardens at each home. Stop for lunch or tea.

The Museum of Garden History located on Lambeth Palace Road in London. It is open Monday through Friday 11:00 to 3:00 and Sunday 10:30 to 5:00 (071 373 4030).

Of course there is always Nottingham Castle, Sherwood Forest, Windsor Castle, Eton College, Ascott Park, Wimbledon and the entire city of London.

Levens Hall Garden

TOURS
from
LONDON to
THE LAKE DISTRICT

TOUR #1
MAP

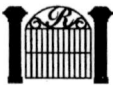

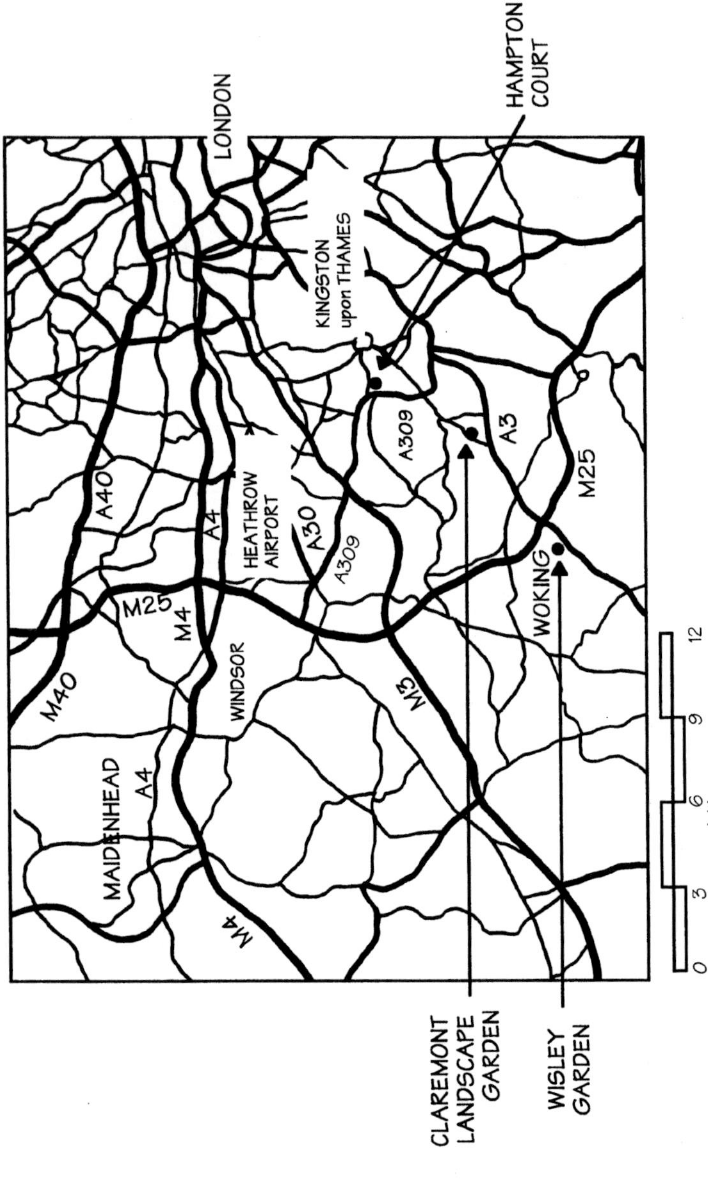
LONDON
HAMPTON COURT
KINGSTON upon THAMES
A40
A4
HEATHROW AIRPORT
A30
A309
A309
A3
M25
WOKING
M25
M4
WINDSOR
M40
M3
MAIDENHEAD
A4
M4
CLAREMONT LANDSCAPE GARDEN
WISLEY GARDEN
0
3
6
9
12
Miles

TOUR #1

* CLAREMONT LANDSCAPE GARDEN
* HAMPTON COURT
* WISLEY GARDEN

• DAILY •

In this tour you will find three wonderful gardens that cover several centuries and several garden styles. Hampton Court, dating back to the 14th century, was home to the British Monarchy with gardens fit for a King. Claremont, one of the earliest landscape gardens, was touched by several great designers of the 18th century. Finally, the world famous gardens at Wisley may provide ideas for your own garden. At least two hours are needed for each of these gardens. Travel time between Hampton Court and Wisley is 20 minutes. Travel time between Wisley and Claremont is 20 minutes.

CLAREMONT LANDSCAPE GARDEN (N.T.)
- Hours of Admission: 10:00 to 6:00
- Location: south edge of Esher, east side of A307
  - One of earliest surviving English landscape gardens was one of the most famous in Europe during the 18th Century.
  - It was begun by John Vanbrugh who purchased the site in 1708, further developed by Charles Bridgeman and extended and naturalized by William Kent and "Capability" Brown between 1711 and 1774.
  - The glorious turf amphitheater that looks down on the lake was designed by Charles Bridgeman in 1726.
  - Rhododendrons surround the lake and island pavilion built by William Kent. Relax and watch the black swans swim peacefully by.
  - VanBrugh built the splendid "medieval" style belvedere.
  - "Capability" Brown was also commissioned to rebuild the house and make improvements to the grounds.
  - The 50 acre estate was acquired by the National Trust in 1949 and, with donations from several sources, restored to its former glory between 1975 & 1980.
  - Note: Not fancy but a historical landscape typical of 18th century.

Hampton Court

HAMPTON COURT
- Hours of Admission: 9:30 to 6:00
- Location: on the A309 just off A3 at Kingston
- This historic palace is located on a spectacular site, an inside curve of the Thames.
- Built for Cardinal Wolsey in the 1500's, it was annexed by Henry VIII in 1525.
- The 16th century gardens, lying between palace and river, were modest in scale.
- In the 17th century, under restored Charles II, they took on a baroque style with a central canal and lime avenues radiating from the house.
- Starting in 1689, William & Mary enlisted the aid of Sir Christopher Wren to make several fabulous additions to the palace and to the garden including the famous yew-maze. The garden took on more of the grand scale of Versailles.
- The Great Fountain Garden, designed during the William & Mary reign, is one of the most spectacular parts of the pleasure grounds. It is designed in a semi-circle with thirteen fountains.
- King William's four great parterres, probably designed by Huguenot artist Daniel Marot, were destroyed during Queen Anne's reign.
- George II, who died in 1760, was the last monarch to live here. He engaged both William Kent and Charles Bridgeman who swept away much of the formal garden.
- Under George III, 'Capability' Brown added his touch. The grounds began to take on the character of a public park.
- In 1838 Queen Victoria opened the palace and grounds to the public.
- Many parts of the garden you see today are truly 20th century in style.
- In the Pond Garden (area between palace and the Thames) you will find cone shaped yews forming an allee leading to a fountain. Mixed borders along the base of the palace provide a fabulous mixture of foliage colors, shapes and sizes as well as flowers.
- The Privy Garden has been restored to its 1701 glory. One of most elaborate and impeccably researched pieces of garden restoration ever undertaken in England.
- One of my favorite areas is the Sunken Garden. A riot of color in the spring is provided by hundreds of bulbs, especially tulips. In summer perennials such as salvias, verbena, geraniums again produce a wonderful array of color.
- Naturally, another one of my favorite features is the walled rose garden. A wonderful collection of teas.
- Look for the Tudor design knot garden with clipped box hedges and beautiful begonias.
- Note: I found the assorted patterns of brickwork on the collection of chimneys fascinating. A carriage ride is available, expensive but worthwhile if you want to see it all. Busy, busy place!

Fabulous lily pond at Wisley Garden.

WISLEY GARDEN

- Hours of Admission: 10:00 to 7:00
- Location: off A3 near Woking
- This is the world famous 240 acre garden of the Royal Horticultural Society.
- It was begun in the 1870's when Mr. G.F. Wilson purchased 60 acres and created the famous wild garden and constructed the ponds.
- The Society moved here in 1904 and retained the wild garden, specimen trees and shrubs.
- A great collection of rhododendrons and azaleas were planted on Battleston Hill starting in 1937.
- A large terraced lily pond is filled with hundreds of water lilies all precisely labeled. The design is fabulous and might give you some good ideas for your own garden.
- The extensive rock garden, built up the side of a hill, was constructed in 1911. As you wind your way up the path, you can inspect a terrific collection of plants while you listen to the water falls tumbling over the large boulders that form the backbone of the garden.
- Surrounded by hedges of hornbeam and rosemary, the herb garden has a sundial at its center with four paths radiating from it. Of the four sections, one is devoted to culinary herbs, two to aromatic, three to medical and four to dye plants and folklore associations.
- The huge rose garden is divided into four planting beds set up by color (red, pink, white & yellow). You will find all sorts of roses from climbers on the wooded trellises to tree roses to shrubs to teas. Fabulous climbing roses also cover the rope trellises lining both sides.
- Among the other features you will find a formal rose garden, an alpine meadow full of wild flowers and bulbs in the spring and two walled gardens designed by Geoffrey Jellicoe.
- There are two restaurants, a picnic area, a visitor center which contains the world's best selection of gardening books and a garden center with over 8500 varieties of plants for sale.
- Note: This place is a must but it can get a little crazy! Thousands of visitors stop here every day. Best time to visit would be during the week.

OTHER GARDENS IN THE AREA: THE SAVILLE GARDEN, KEW GARDENS

TOUR #2
MAP

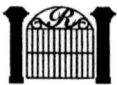

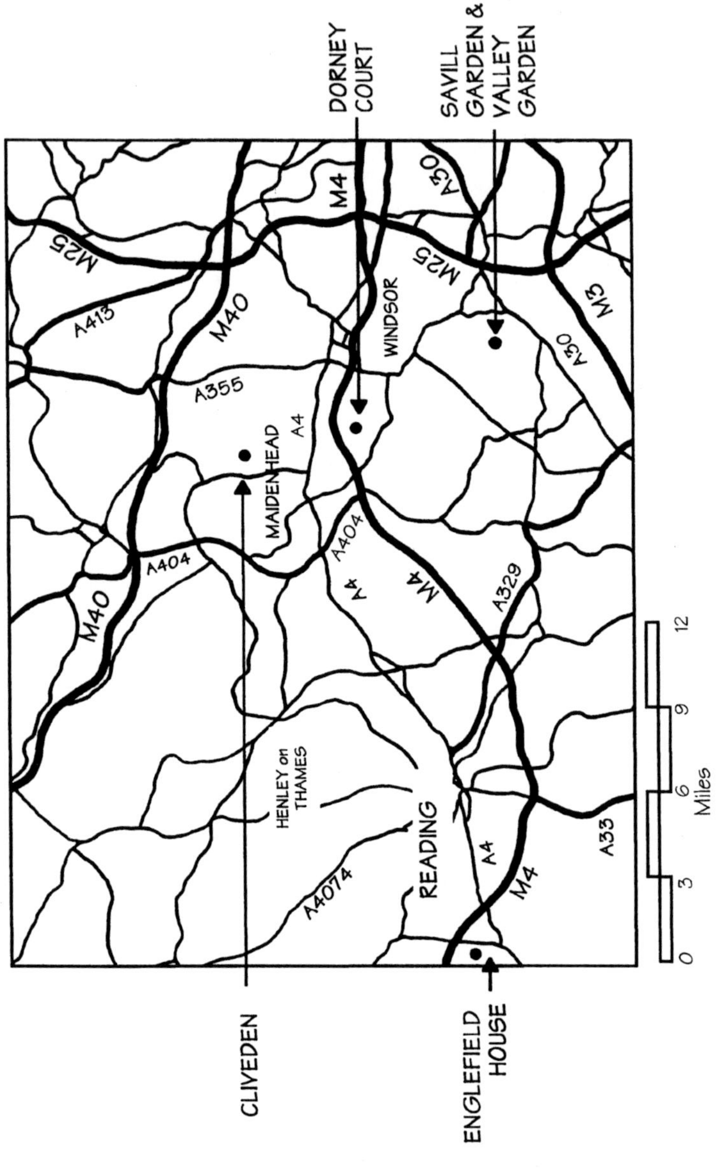

DORNEY COURT
SAVILL GARDEN & VALLEY GARDEN
M4
A30
M25
M40
A413
A355
WINDSOR
M3
MAIDENHEAD
A4
A404
A329
HENLEY on THAMES
READING
A4074
A33
0
3
6
9
12
Miles
CLIVEDEN
ENGLEFIELD HOUSE

TOUR #2

* ENGLEFIELD HOUSE
* THE SAVILL GARDEN
* CLIVEDEN

• MONDAY THROUGH THURSDAY •

Looking for unusual borders and beautiful woodlands? Savill Gardens/ Valley Garden is the place for you. Two to three hours, at least, will be needed here. You need to drive a little out of your way to visit Englefield House but this well designed terraced garden is worth it. Last stop is the fabulous Astor estate at Cliveden. After you have enjoyed the formal garden, you might even want to spend the night. One to two hours are need for Englefield and Cliveden. Travel time between Savill and Englefield is at least an hour. Travel time between Englefield and Cliveden is also an hour.

ENGLEFIELD HOUSE
- Hours of Admission: 10:00 to dusk
- Location: 4 miles west of Reading off A4 and then 3/4 mile on A340
  - Enjoy the long drive that leads to this imposing manor house. The seven acre garden and Deer Park provide a beautiful setting.
  - As you approach the house you will pass a charming little church with red roses blooming in front.
  - A series of terraces are edged with fabulous stone railings and highlighted by large colorfully planted pots settled on top. Mixed borders are created by selecting plants for foliage contrasts as well as colorful roses and perennials. These terraces also provide a good place to enjoy wonderful views out to the countryside.
  - The unusual children's garden is very sweet. It looks like it was designed for the family children and is truly a part of the garden, not the colorful climbing things we usually see.
  - Look for a little piece of home, a giant sequoia which is 150-200 years old.
  - Walk up behind the terraced area and you will find a stream with boggy planting that provides interesting color and foliage contrasts. There are also great Japanese maples, big English oaks and many other large shade trees.
  - If you are visiting in spring, be sure to take the woodland walk.
  - Note: Nice surprise. Well designed garden, worth visiting even though it is somewhat out of the way. Home not open to the public.

THE SAVILL GARDEN

- Hours of Admission: 10:00 to 6:00
- Location: Wick Lane, signposted from Ascot & Windsor
- Set in Windsor Great Park, this thirty-five acre world-renowned woodland garden was laid out in this century.
- Eric Savill, whose strengths were in his landscape ability and his great love of good plants, took up the duties of Deputy Surveyor in 1932. In 1951 King George VI honored him by renaming the garden Savill Garden.
- You will find beauty in all seasons. In spring you will find daffodils and bluebells, and fragrant philadelphus. In summer there is a wonderful collection of roses and colorful herbaceous plants. Even autumn brings the glorious reds, yellows and oranges of liquidamber, Japanese maples and many more.
- Queen Elizabeth Temperate House was constructed in 1994 and named for the Queen Mother. It is very well done in both architecture and planting. Built to house tender plants, those sensitive to the colder English climate.
- Borders are longer and wider than most and accommodate much larger plants. This is an opportunity to see many wonderful plants too large to grow in your own garden. I was really impressed with the scale and presentation of plant material.
- The Raised Beds, a lovely and interesting corner, is sheltered by walls built of bricks from London buildings destroyed in the blitz.
- A large boggy area along the ponds are again large in scale with huge hostas and astillbes, big old ferns and many other big leafed plants.
- Valley Garden is within walking distance of Savill Garden and part of Windsor Great Park. Development began in 1947 by Sir Eric Savill.
- Four hundred acres of woodlands are endowed with large shade trees, rare rhododendrons, flowering trees, huge magnolias and fabulous camellias.
- For color in summer, hydrangeas are used widely throughout the garden including several acres of breathtaking color in the Hydrangea Garden.
- Note: Plants are well identified. Stop and enjoy lunch or tea at the lovely restaurant, the outdoor seating is great on those sunny days. See how many different agapanthus you can identify. I loved the very tiny 'Liliput'.

Fountain at Cliveden.

Garden Tours of England

Colorful pots decorate the stone railings at Englefield House.

CLIVEDEN (N.T.)
- Hours of Admission: 11:00 to 6:30
- Location: 4 miles north of Maidenhead on A4094
- Present house, built in 1851, was designed by Sir Charles Barry, the designer of The House of Parliament. It was purchased in 1893 by American, William Waldorf Astor.
- This 18th century landscape of one hundred and eighty acres looks over the Thames Valley.
- Incredible Fountain of Love stands at the end of the linden lined avenue. A huge marble shell provides the background for several cavorting cupids. Very romantic!
- The Long Garden reflects Lord Astor's love for Italian Renaissance gardens from the terrace balustrade taken from the Villa Borghese in Rome to the design and planting of the parterre. This unbelievable parterre is twenty acres of simple, very formal planting. You should stand on the terrace to truly appreciate the scope of the parterre and lovely views to the countryside in all three directions.
- Charles Bridgeman created the amphitheater in 1723.
- Herbaceous borders were planted in Gertrude Jekyll style.
- You will also find a Rose Garden, designed by Geoffrey Jellicoe in 1959, planted with shrub roses and arch covered climbers.
- Over a mile of riverfront and woodland is filled with rhododendrons and bluebells in spring.
- Lord Astor gave to the property to the National Trust in 1942. It was one of the first great houses to be given to the National Trust.
- It became a luxury hotel in 1985. The income provides finances for restoration and maintenance of the gardens and buildings.
- Note: Enjoy lunch in the old orangery. Several colorful planters many give you some good ideas. Fabulous hotel if a little pricy- £265.00 single (01628 668561).

OTHER GARDENS IN THE AREA: HAMPTON COURT, HUGHENDON MANOR, DORNEY COURT

TOUR # 3
MAP

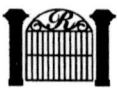

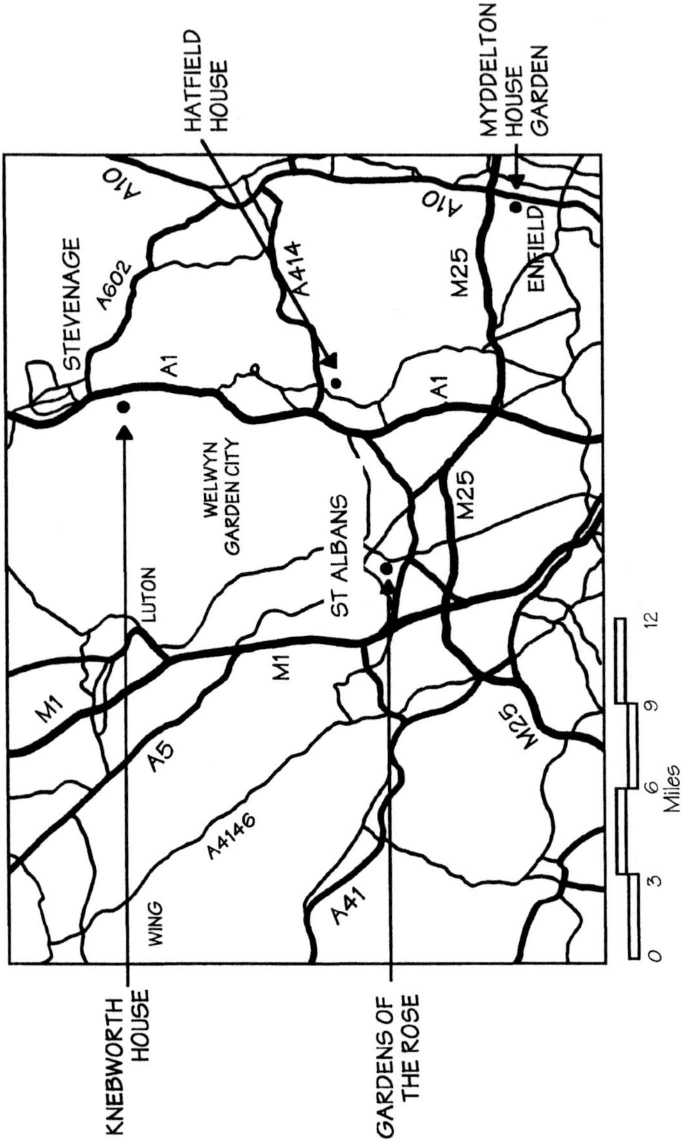
HATFIELD HOUSE
MYDDELTON HOUSE GARDEN
STEVENAGE
A10
A602
A1
A414
M25
ENFIELD
WELWYN GARDEN CITY
ST ALBANS
LUTON
M1
A5
A4146
WING
A41
KNEBWORTH HOUSE
GARDENS OF THE ROSE
0 3 6 9 12
Miles

TOUR #3

* KNEBWORTH HOUSE
* HATFIELD HOUSE
* THE GARDENS OF THE ROSE
* MYDDELTON HOUSE GARDENS

• MONDAY THROUGH FRIDAY •

Lots to see today, no time to dawdle! An imposing 17th century house and a lovely sunken knot garden are only two of the sights awaiting you at Hatfield House. Roses, roses everywhere! Could there be anything better, at St Albans. At least two hours are needed at these two gardens. 19th century gargoyles look down on Gertrude Jekyll's charming herb garden at Knebworth. One to two hours are needed here. Onelast stop, at E.A. Bowles home at Myddelton House. About an hour is needed here. Travel time between Myddelton and St. Albans is 40. Travel time between St. Albans and Hatfield House is 30 minutes. Travel time between Hatfield and Knebworth is 20 minutes.

KNEBWORTH HOUSE
- Hours of Admission: 11:00 to 5:30
- Location: 30 miles north of central London, from A1 at junction 7
- This has been the home of the Lytton family for over 500 years.
- In 1843 High Gothic turrets and gargoyles were added to transform the original Tudor design.
- Frequent visitors to the manor were Charles Dickens who even acted in Jacobean Hall in 1850 and Winston Churchill who painted the Banqueting Hall. That painting hangs in the hall today.
- Formal Victorian gardens were redesigned and simplified by Sir Edwin Lutyens in 1911.
- Gertrude Jekyll designed a charming herb garden in 1907 but planting was never done. The original plans were found in the archives at U.C. Berkeley in 1980 and two years later the herb garden was reconstructed and planted.
- An especially cheerful area is the Yellow Garden. Various shades of yellow are found in both foliage and flowers planted in a circular pattern around a fountain. Nicely done!
- Lovely 'Fairy' roses trained in a canopy of little pink flowers are just one feature of the rose garden. You will also find shrub roses and colorful perennials reflected in two rectangular ponds.
- Be sure to wind your way through the recently reinstated Victorian maze.
- Note: Two hundred and fifty acres of parkland are interesting for a 'short' stroll by the adventuresome and an ideal spot for a family picnic.

Stately Knebworth looks over lovely rose beds.

HATFIELD HOUSE
- Hours of Admission: 11:00 to 6:00
- Location: 21 miles north of London, A1 junction 4
- This wonderful Jacobean house was built between 1607 and 1611 by Robert Cecil, 1st Earl of Salisbury and has been in the family since.
- Within the garden stands the surviving wing of the Royal Palace of Hatfield (1497) where Elizabeth I spent much of her childhood and was confined during her sister Mary's reign.
- Starting in 1607, the head gardener was John Tradescant, the Elder. He was in touch with many of the plant collectors of the time. In 1611 500 fruit trees arrived from the French Queen; in 1612, 453 cherries and 1200 limes came from France.
- The formal gardens were swept away for the parkland style in the mid-18th century. However, in the 1840's, in anticipation of the visit of Queen Victoria much of the formal Jacobean garden was reinstated.
- Since 1972 the Marchioness of Salisbury has used Tradescant's diaries to transform the gardens to their 17th century glory.
- Enjoy the lovely sunken knot garden. It is viewed from the terrace above which is great for pictures and studying the design. The garden is 150 feet square with boxwood hedges and roses and perennials from the 16th and 17th centuries.
- Stone balustrade and a double staircase lead to formal gardens where you will find eight square beds hedged by boxwoods and filled with old fashion roses, herbs and flowering shrubs.
- One of my favorites areas was an enclosed garden. Yew hedges with clever topiaries, enclose colorful beds of roses and perennials in a circular shape around a center fountain and pond.
- Other lovely features you will find include: a simple low growing boxwood maze with soothing water sounds from the center fountain and a very old lime pergola with leaves flashing in the breeze.
- Note: The sunken garden is open one day a week to walk around. The famous east gardens are only open on Mondays from 2:00 to 5:00.

THE GARDENS OF THE ROSE
- Hours of Admission: 9:00 to 5:00
- Location: 2 miles south of St. Albans
  - This wonderful rose garden is the Royal National Rose Society test grounds as well as show grounds for hundreds of varieties of roses. 1,650 varieties, as a matter of fact, and 30,000 plants.
  - You will find many large test beds. Each bed is filled with a specific variety tested for pruning styles, various fertilizers, mulches, watering habits, etc. Could be some interesting information to take back to your own garden.
  - I'm sure you will enjoy the long semi circular pergola covered with pink roses and purple and lavender clematis. It is very special! The pergola partially encloses a charming lily pond surrounded by tiny pink 'Fairy' roses.
  - The town of St. Albans was founded 2000 years ago. The first blood of the War of the Roses was shed in these streets.
  - Note: I've been there at various times of the year. The best time to visit is in July and August. The roses are in glorious bloom with color everywhere.

MYDDELTON HOUSE GARDENS
- Hours of Admission 10:00 to 3:30
- Location: junction of M25 and A10, on Bulls Cross, Enfield
  - This four acre garden containing many rare and unique plants was the creation and the home of famous plantsman, E.A. Bowles.
  - Primarily a spring garden, millions of bulbs and the National Collection of Award Winning Bearded Iris create a riot of color.
  - One of the nicest features is a large pond area with water lilies and lush planting around the edges. Stone steps provide two terrace levels and a charming greenhouse on the upper terrace.
  - Note: Historically significant. The structure and much of the plant material remains from Bowles original creation. Unfortunately the maintenance was very disappointing.

Charming fountain is surrounded by colorful beds at Hatfield House.

OTHER GARDENS IN THE AREA: WREST PARK HOUSE, SWISS GARDEN, ASCOTT, CAPEL MANOR

TOUR #4
MAP

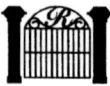

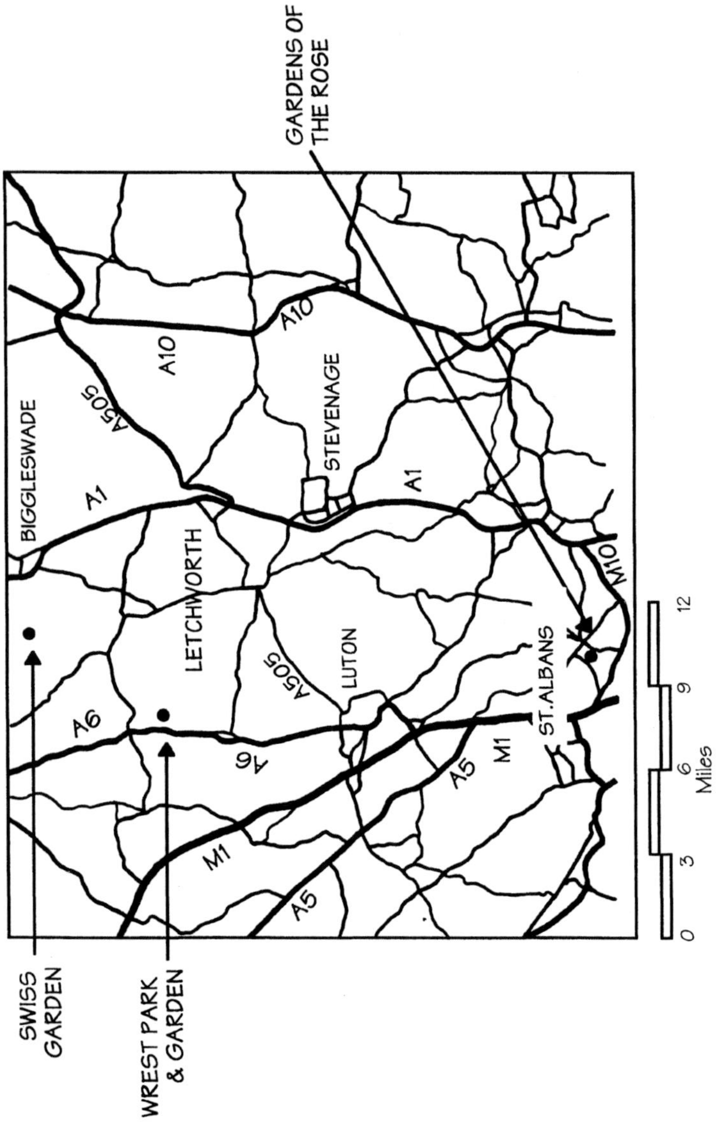

GARDENS OF
THE ROSE
BIGGLESWADE
A505
A10
A10
A10
STEVENAGE
A1
A1
LETCHWORTH
A505
LUTON
ST. ALBANS
M10
A6
A6
M1
M1
A5
A5
0
3
6
9
12
Miles
SWISS
GARDEN
WREST PARK
& GARDEN

TOUR #4

* THE GARDENS OF THE ROSE
* SWISS GARDEN
* WREST PARK & GARDENS

• SATURDAY & SUNDAY •

The 18th century canal, Long Water, is laid out in front of the fabulous Pavilion at Wrest Park. A spring garden filled with bulbs and rhododendrons and charming thatched roofs highlight the gardens at Swiss Garden. One to two hours are needed at each of these gardens. Enjoy the glorious color of thousands of roses at St. Albans. I always find a few that are musts for my own garden. When the roses are in full bloom you will need at least two hours to properly enjoy. Travel time between St. Albans and Wrest Park is 45 minutes. Travel time between Wrest Park and Swiss Garden is 20 minutes.

THE GARDENS OF THE ROSE
- Hours of Admission: 9:00 to 5:00
- Location: 2 miles south of St. Albans
- This wonderful rose garden is the Royal National Rose Society test grounds as well as show grounds for hundreds of varieties of roses. 1,650 varieties, as a matter of fact, and 30,000 plants.
- You will find many large test beds. Each bed is filled with a specific variety tested for pruning styles, various fertilizers, mulches, watering habits, etc. Could be some interesting information to take back to your own garden.
- I'm sure you will enjoy the long semi circular pergola covered with pink roses and purple and lavender clematis. It is very special! The pergola partially encloses a charming lily pond surrounded by tiny pink 'Fairy' roses.
- The town of St. Albans was founded 2000 years ago. The first blood of the War of the Roses was shed in these streets.
- Note: I've been there at various times of the year. The best time to visit is in July and August. The roses are in glorious bloom with color everywhere.

Intricate green iron bridge at Swiss Garden.

Cone shaped topoaries and roses, roses, roses at St. Albans.

SWISS GARDEN
- Hours of Admission: wknds 10:00 to 6:00, wkdays 1:30 to 6:00
- Location: 1.5 miles west of Biggleswade A1 roundabout
  - The early 19th century design was inspired by all things Swiss as was the fashion in 1820's England, thus the name Swiss Garden. Early planting was simple, ponds were dug and the dirt was used to create dips and mounds.
  - In the 1870's, the new owner Joseph Shuttleworth rebuilt the mansion in the style of the day, gothic. He made few changes to the garden except to add a few Victorian touches.
  - Over 40 years, beginning during World War II, the garden was left to deteriorate.
  - Starting in 1976 restoration began and the garden was once more opened to the public in 1981.
  - The charming thatched roofed Swiss Cottage was built in the 1820's.
  - Look for the thatched tree bench built around one of the broadest oak trees you may ever see. A good place to take a moment to rest and enjoy the view.
  - Stained glass doors lead you to the Grotto and Fernery. From the gloom and mystery of the grotto you move to the dazzling light of the fernery. Here you will find an early use of cast-iron in English glass houses-produced between 1830-1833.
  - This is largely a spring garden; a woodland garden filled with masses of daffodils and lush rhododendrons and azaleas.
  - The garden is located a distance from the mansion and designed to heighten a visitors anticipation.
  - Note: A charming garden experiencing continuing restoration. Plan on plenty of walking. Look out for free roaming cows. They greeted us at the entry.

WREST PARK & GARDENS

- Hours of Admission: 10:00 to 6:00
- Location: 1 mile east of Silsoe off A6
  - This wonderful 19th century mansion was built in the style of an 18th century French chateau.
  - Many gardens have gone through several changes over the years but Wrest is one of the best examples of changing styles between 1700-1850.
  - The French Garden, a formal parterre with a marble fountain leads you to a broad expanse of lawn and the dominant feature of the garden.
  - In the Great Garden, laid out between 1706 and 1740, you will find a magnificent canal, Long Water and a fabulous Pavilion designed by Thomas Archer between 1709 and 1711. The design provides several points of interest and vistas in all directions. Extensive woodland gardens flank the Great Garden.
  - A fine early 19th century Orangery was designed by Earl de Gray and is found to the west of the French Garden.
  - 'Capability' Brown was hired to naturalize the landscape but fortunately many of the early 18th century features remain.
  - Be sure to see the rustic stone bath house built in an 18th century style. This must have been quite a little spa in its day. Soothing water sounds from the cascade nearby fill the air.
  - Note: First impression of the property- a complex of more modern buildings where business meetings are conducted. Look past this. As you enter the garden you will be transformed back in time. A part of the English Heritage.

One of the beautiful sculptures to be enjoyed at Wrest Park.

OTHER GARDENS IN THE AREA: KNEBWORTH HOUSE, HATFIELD HOUSE, MYDDELTON HOUSE, CAPEL MANOR

TOUR #5
MAP

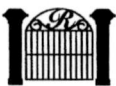

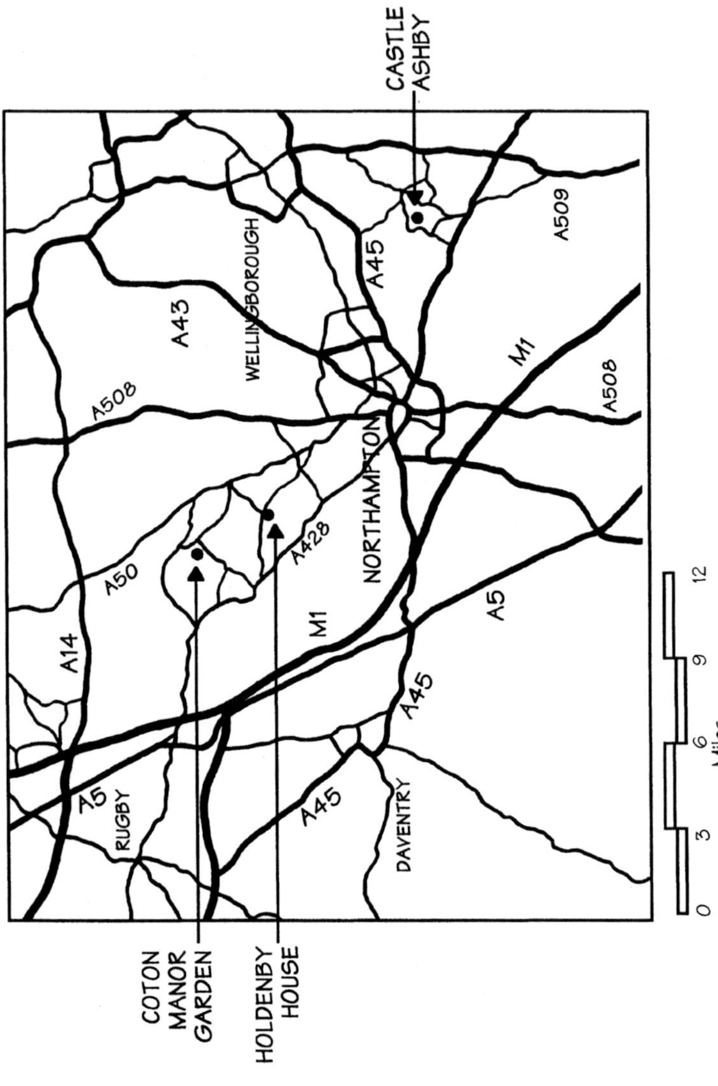

CASTLE ASHBY
WELLINGBOROUGH
NORTHAMPTON
RUGBY
DAVENTRY
A43
A45
A508
A509
M1
A50
A428
A14
A5
COTON MANOR GARDEN
HOLDENBY HOUSE
0
3
6
9
12
Miles

Garden Tours of England

TOUR #5
* CASTLE ASHBY
* COTON MANOR GARDEN
* HOLDENBY HOUSE

• WEDNESDAY, THURSDAY, FRIDAY, SUNDAY•

I love surprises and Coton Manor was a pleasant one! Colorful borders filled with roses and perennials, a lovely pond and a charming stone house will provide two to three hours of pleasure. 16th and 17th century royal history and a fragrant herb garden designed by Rosemary Verey await you at Holdenby House. Enjoy the romantic feeling of the cone shaped topiaries, roses and colorful stone pots in the formal Italian garden at Castle Ashby. Up to two hours are needed at these two gardens. Travel time between Castle Ashby and Holdenby House is 45 minutes. Travel time between Holdenby and Coton Manor is 15 minutes.

CASTLE ASHBY
- Hours of Admission: 10:00 to 5:00
- Location: 6 miles east of Northampton, 1.5 miles north of A428
- This property has been in the Compton family since 1512 when it was given to them by Henry VIII.
- The original 13th century castle was demolished and rebuilt starting in 1574. In honor of Queen Elizabeth I, the castle was built in an 'E' shape. The courtyard has since been enclosed.
- The lettering around the roof line is an interesting and unusual feature. It translates, "The Lord guard your coming in." and "The Lord guard your going out."
- The garden is a combination of styles.
- An exceptionally long avenue dating to 1695 leads up to the castle. Watch out for the free grazing sheep.
- The yew hedges, cone shaped topiaries, roses and stone pots overflowing with color give the formal Italian Garden a very romantic feeling.
- A lovely stone and glass Conservatory provides shelter for many tender plants. Look for the interesting siral staircase leading to the roof.
- You will also find a Victorian Terrace Garden, a 'Capability' Brown parkland and I even discovered a purple leaf beech that must be 200 years old.

Castle Ashby

COTON MANOR GARDEN
- Hours of Admission: 12:00 to 6:00
- Location: 9 miles north of Northampton off A428
- I love surprises and this was a very pleasant one!
- A 17th century stone farmhouse and surrounding farmland were purchased by the Bryant family in 1925. With the existing building as the southern wing, the house was rebuilt and added on to create the charming stone manor house seen today.
- Main portions of the garden were established in the 1920's and 1930's but it fell into disrepair during World War II.
- Parents of current owner, Commander & Mrs. Pasley-Tyler came to live here and started restoration on the property in 1950. She had a flair for plants which complemented the Commander's talent for landscaping and water engineering.
- The property was opened to the public in 1969 to help defray the cost of maintaining and to eventually expanding the garden.
- Greeting you on arrival is the Commander's son, the owner since 1990. He is happy to answer questions and talk about the garden while his wife can frequently be found working in the garden.
- You will find a beautifully designed garden laid out on several levels or terraces.
- Stone paving with narrow borders, vines growing on the stone house and big pots of colorful flowers provide the connection between the house and the garden.
- Pink and white roses and peonies abound in the lovely rose garden. A pretty stone urn provides the centerpiece. Look for two of my favorite roses, 'Felicia' and 'Penelope'.
- The glorious main border, backed by an old holly hedge, is primarily herbaceous with a few shrub roses. A wonderful mixture of plants provides color from spring to fall.
- Larger in scale, the lower border is designed to display bolder colors and plants with greater height and larger foliage. This spot also provides an opportunity to look back at the pond, upper borders and house.
- Relax for a few minutes in the summerhouse and enjoy the sights and soothing sounds of the water garden. A canopy of large trees provides shade for a fabulous array of plants.
- Note: This little known garden was wonderful and I'm anxious to return soon. Can you find the infamous 'pink flamingos'? Be sure to stop for a homemade tea.

16th century gateway at Holdenby House.

Garden Tours of England

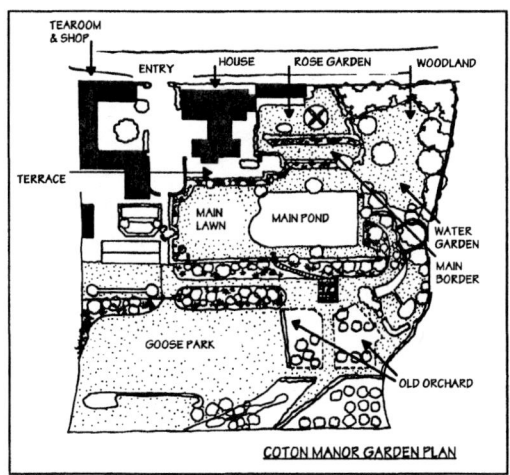

HOLDENBY HOUSE
- Hours of Admission: 2:00 to 6:00
- Location: 6 miles northwest of Northampton off A428
- Originally built in 1583, it was once a great Renaissance palace and the largest house in England.
- The garden was created by Sir Christopher Hatton, Lord Chancellor and an intimate to Queen Elizabeth I.
- Remnants of the original design still survive including a series of terraces and a pair of stone and brick arched gateways dating from 1583.
- King Charles I was imprisoned here for five months in 1647 following his defeat in the Civil War. The house was largely demolished after his execution, then rebuilt. Additions were made in the 19th century which resulted in the house you see today.
- The charming Elizabethan garden was planted by Rosemary Verey in 1980. A variety of fragrant herbs provide color in a circular pattern around a sun dial and the surrounding yew hedges give the character of a secret garden.
- Look for a fine kitchen garden with a small greenhouse. The fruits and vegetables are mixed with an assortment of colorful roses.
- The Falconry Center gives you the opportunity to try this traditional royal pursuit. Take a few minutes to enjoy the many different kinds of birds on display and one of the demonstrations held each day.
- Note: Several craftsmen have shops in the courtyard. Even one of my favorites-Windsor chairs.

OTHER GARDENS IN THE AREA: COTTESBROOKE HALL

TOUR # 6
MAP

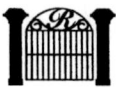

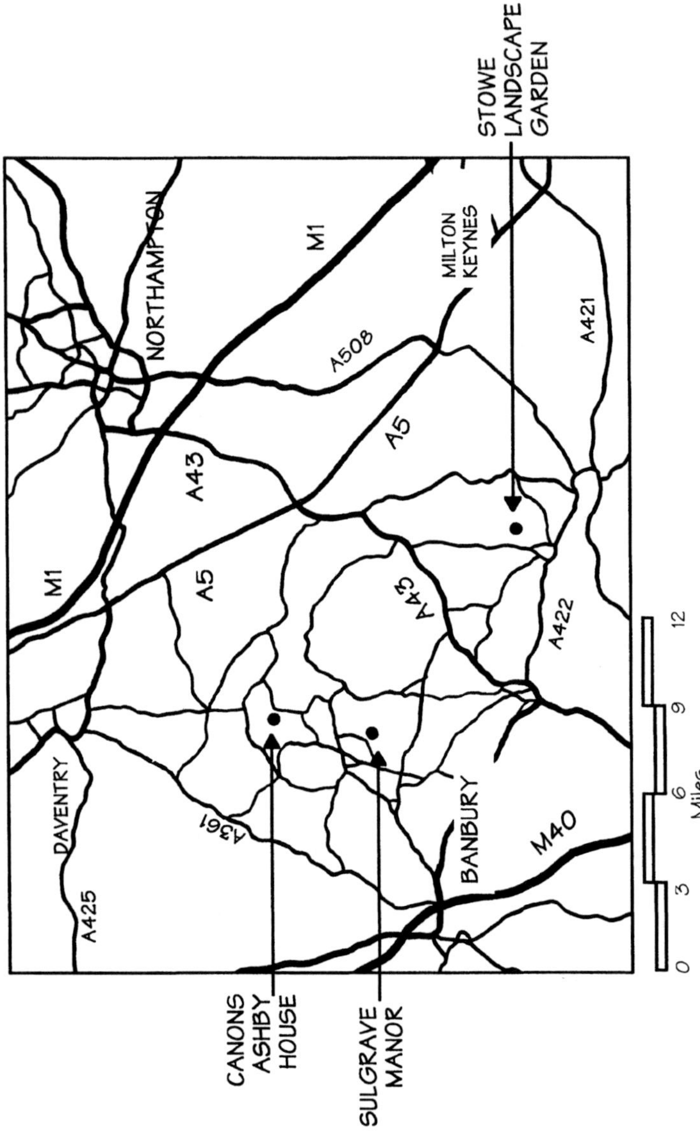

STOWE
LANDSCAPE
GARDEN
NORTHAMPTON
M1
MILTON
KEYNES
A508
A421
A5
A43
A5
A43
M1
A422
DAVENTRY
A361
BANBURY
M40
A425
CANONS
ASHBY
HOUSE
SULGRAVE
MANOR
0
3
6
9
12
Miles

TOUR #6

* SULGRAVE MANOR
* STOWE LANDSCAPE GARDEN
* CANONS ASHBY HOUSE

• SATURDAY THROUGH TUESDAY •

A little American history and the ties that bind the 'Colonies' to England are found at the Washington residence, Sulgrave Manor. At Canons Ashby House charming topiaries and rose filled terraces give you a real taste of the original 18th century beauty of this garden. One to two hours are needed at both Sulgrave and Canons Ashby. Plan on a fair amount of walking and at least two hours in the fabulous landscape garden at Stowe. This garden was touched by many of the famous designers of the 18th century. Travel time between Sulgrave and Canons Ashby is 20 minutes. Travel time between Canons Ashby and Stowe is 40 minutes.

SULGRAVE MANOR
- Hours of Admission: 2:00 to 5:30
- Location: 7 miles from junction 11 of M40 off B4525
  - Built in the 16th century by Lawrence Washington, this was the early English home of George Washington's ancestors. Now be patient, Lawrence was great-great-grandfather of John Washington who emigrated to Virginia in 1657. John was great-grandfather of George.
  - Restored, it is good example of a small manor house during the time of William Shakespeare.
  - Washington family coat of arms, registered in 1346, is seen at the front door. It is said to have inspired the Stars and Strips of the American flag.
  - Sulgrave was in need of extensive renovations in the early 20th century and in 1914 both British and American subscribers raised the money needed to restore and preserve the house. It was opened to the public in 1921.
  - The attractive gardens were designed in 1921 by Sir Reginald Blomfield.
  - Note: In the summer of 1998 the grounds were undergoing major reconstruction. Look for good things in spring 1999.

The original flag adopted by the thirteen colonies.

39

Stately Palladian Bridge at Stowe Landscape Garden.

STOWE LANDSCAPE GARDEN (N.T.)
- Hours of Admission: 10:00 to 5:00
- Location: 3 miles northwest of Buckingham off A422
- This may be the most important landscape garden in Britain. It is one of the supreme creations of the Georgian era.
- Initially formal in design, Sir Richard Temple (Viscount Cobham) began construction in the 16th century. It took 40 years and a great deal of money to achieve his goal.
- In the 18th century the Temple family employed many leading architects, landscape architects & sculptors. Vanbrugh, Bridgeman, Kent and Brown were all involved in designing the garden.
- Between 1714 and 1720 Charles Bridgeman laid out formal gardens to the south of the house.
- See if you can find the 30 garden buildings (temples, obelisks, a grotto and a shell bridge) designed by William Kent.
- One of the most impressive sights is the Elysian Fields which was also designed by William Kent.
- "Capability" Brown (head gardener from 1741 to 1751), recreated the rolling hills, woods and lakes in the new naturalistic style of the period.
- Bankruptcy in 1848 forced the sale of the contents of the house and the estate was sold in 1920 and turned into a school.
- The National Trust acquired the property in 1989 and has embarked on one of the most ambitious and expensive programs of garden restoration ever undertaken in Britain; a restoration that will take more than 10 years.
- Note: Very interesting and worth seeing. Much of the restoration has been completed.

CANONS ASHBY HOUSE (N.T.)

- Hours of Admission: 1:00 to 5:30
- Location: 2 miles south of Weedon crossroads off A5
  - The home of the Dryden family since the 16th century, the manor was built c. 1550 and was altered several times over the years to the house you see today.
  - You will find one of the best surviving formal garden layouts in the style of Henry London and George Wise and a seventy acre park.
  - There are small borders along stone walls, yew hedges, charming topiaries and terraces with colorful roses.
  - Gate piers dated 1710 lead you to views of the beautiful countryside and a lovely lake below.
  - Derelict and overgrown when rescued by National Trust, the garden was restored between 1980 and 1984.
  - Note: This is a simple, well maintained garden. The house is also worth exploring.

Sheep roam freely at Canons Ashby.

OTHER GARDENS IN THE AREA: COTON MANOR GARDEN, HOLDENBY HOUSE

TOUR #7
MAP

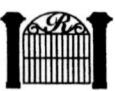

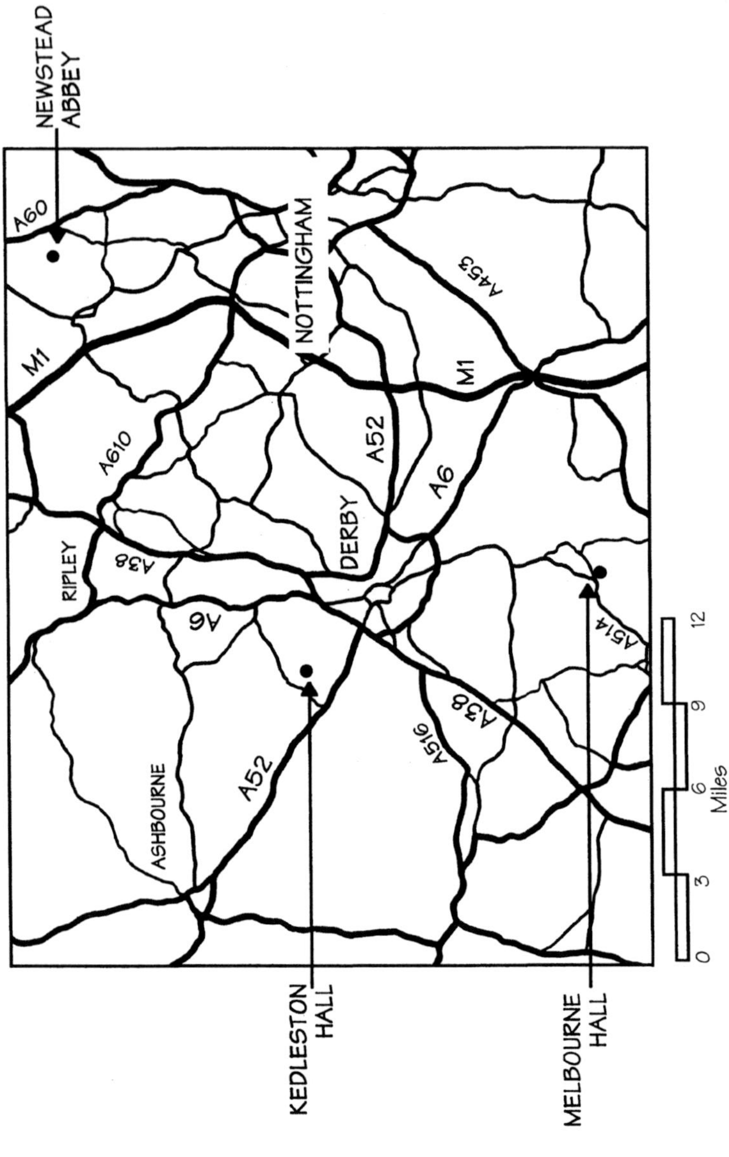

NEWSTEAD ABBEY
A60
NOTTINGHAM
A453
M1
M1
A610
A52
A6
DERBY
RIPLEY
A38
A6
A514
A38
A516
A52
ASHBOURNE
KEDLESTON HALL
MELBOURNE HALL
0
3
6
9
12
Miles

TOUR #7

* MELBOURNE HALL
* KEDLESTON HALL
* NEWSTEAD ABBEY

• SATURDAY, SUNDAY, WEI

The villas of Italian architect Palladio inspired the fabulous Kedleston Hall. From the house you can enjoy the beautiful countryside and the 18th century landscape garden. Another 18th century garden can be found at Melbourne Hall. This time, a formal style by Henry Wise. Next lets visit the home of poet, Lord Byron. At Newstead Abbey you will find a lovely lake, glorious old fashioned roses and a 20th century Japanese garden. At least two hours will be needed at each garden. Travel time between Melbourne and Kedleston is 30 minutes. Travel time between Kedleston and Newstead Abbey is about one hour.

MELBOURNE HALL
- Hours of Admission: 2:00 to 6:00
  - Location: 8 miles south of Derby on A514
    - May be the only existing formal Henry Wise garden of the early 18th century left in England; others were lost to landscape phase.
    - On a modest scale, ten acres, it was referred to as 'the formal garden grown informal and English'.
    - In his design Wise incorporated several statues by John Van Nost, the foremost garden sculptor of the time. The imposing Four Seasons Monument, a gift from Queen Anne and a charming pair of cherubs are only two.
    - The terraced lawn leads to the Great Basin which spreads out before the exquisite wrought iron domed 'Birdcage', created by the famous ironsmith Robert Bakewell in 1706.
    - 200 yards of yews create a tunnel of gnarled trunks and a 'grumpy' hedge that is older by many years than the garden.
    - Note: The essential structure of the garden still exists. You can see the axial points, allees and vistas but it is overgrown and much of the design is lost.

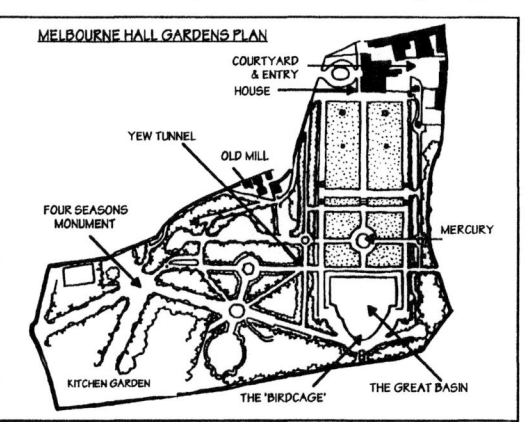

KEDLESTON HALL (N.T.)

Hours of Admission: 11:00 to 6:00
- Location: 5 miles northwest of Derby on A52
  - The design of this fabulous neo-classical house was based on the villas of the Italian architect Palladio. Built between 1759 and 1765, the rooms in central block are furnished and decorated just as they were in 1765.
  - This is an excellent example of a garden designed in the natural style of 'Capability' Brown. Today the eight hundred acres of parkland, laid out in the 1760's, appear to be much like it was in the mid-18th century. Enjoy the sun sparkling on the water as it falls over the cascade into the lake.
  - Laid out between 1761-1776, the 3.5 mile Long Walk, swings round to the south side of the house giving extensive views to the beautiful countryside. The planting is simple with ornamental shrubs and beds of flowers.
  - The pleasure grounds were formalized by Edwin Lutyens and Gertrude Jekyll in early 20th century. Within these pleasure grounds you will find several 18th century garden buildings including an orangery and hexagonal summerhouse.
  - The property was acquired by the National Trust in 1987.
  - Note: A must see for the beauty and historical significance. A good place for a picnic, you can even share your lunch with the sheep.

18th century summerhouse is part of the
Pleasure Grounds at Kedleston Hall.

Swans enjoy the beautiful lake at Newstead Abbey.

NEWSTEAD ABBEY
- Hours of Admission: 9:00 to 6:00
- Location: 12 miles north of Nottingham along A60
- Founded as a prior between 1163 and 1173, this was the historic home of poet, Lord Byron.
- Water flows into the beautiful garden lake through an ornamental cascade. An interesting view of the Abbey and garden is from behind the cascade through the 'window' of water.
- The old walled kitchen garden is now the rose garden, designed in a symmetrical pattern with a fountain and glorious old-fashioned roses.
- Be adventuresome and wander out from the walled garden. Walk around the lake to the entrance to the Japanese garden.
- Early 20th century Japanese garden is well designed with stepping stones, humpbacked bridges, Japanese maples and a lovely assortment of lush plants.
- In early summer a large iris garden is a riot of color. The beds are bordered by boxwood hedges and shaded by old pear trees.
- Stroll behind the abbey and you will find flower beds surrounding a large sunken pool. On the terrace level above, several large trees decorate a wide expanse of lawn. To one side of the terrace, a colorful mixed border lines the wonderful brick and stone wall which extends 150-200 yards.
- Another interesting feature is the sunken Spanish garden. The design is formal; an old well is surrounded by boxwood hedges and several small beds of annuals (marigolds in summer).

OTHER GARDENS IN THE AREA: HARDWICK HALL, CALKE ABBEY, CLUMBER PARK

TOUR # 8
MAP

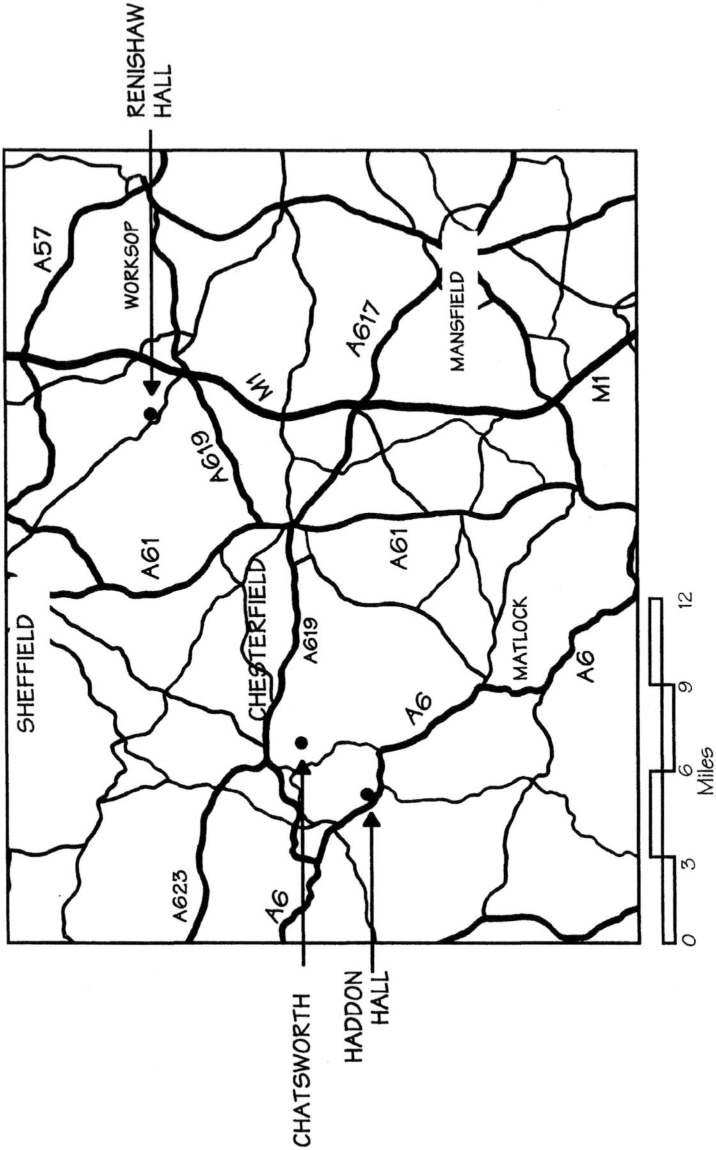
RENISHAW HALL
A57
WORKSOP
A617
MANSFIELD
M1
M1
A619
A61
A61
SHEFFIELD
CHESTERFIELD
A619
MATLOCK
A6
A6
A623
A6
CHATSWORTH
HADDON HALL
0
3
6
9
12
Miles

TOUR #8
* HADDON HALL
* CHATSWORTH
* RENISHAW HALL

• FRIDAY, SATURDAY, SUNDAY •

Big day ahead! Three fabulous gardens. Start with a nice surprise at Renishaw Hall. A series of terraces, rambling roses and a collection of Italian statues display the designers passion for the Italian Renaissance. Next, the romance of Haddon Hall. Roses are a specialty in this 18th century terraced garden that surrounds a medieval manor. Two hours are needed at each. Last stop is at Chatsworth. There is so much to see, plan on a great deal of walking and at least three hours. Travel time between Renishaw and Haddon is 30 minutes. Travel time between Haddon and Chatsworth is 10 minutes.

HADDON HALL
- Hours of Admission: 11:00 to 5:45
- Location: 2.5 miles southeast of Bakewell on A6
  - What you see today is the most complete surviving medieval manor house in England. Haddon Hall has been on this site since before the Domesday survey in 1087. Sited on an outcrop overlooking the River Wye, it has been the home of Manners and Vernon families since 12th century.
  - The garden is entered through a portion of the house and down a flight of worn stone steps constructed in 1649.
  - Although there are records of the garden dating back to the late 16th century, the present garden dates back to the early 18th century. In the early 20th century a massive clearance and replanting was needed in this horribly overgrown garden.
  - The terraced rose garden has been created from stones quarried locally (Cotswold stone look). The walls drop down 18-24 feet to the River Wye below. Look down and you will find a lovely waterfall.
  - Roses are definitely a specialty! Castle walls, balustrades edging the terraces and staircases make perfect places for climbing roses intermingled with clematis. You will find over 150 varieties of roses including many that are seventy years old. What a fabulous riot of color and fragrance!
  - Look for a very special rose, 'Mary Manners', named after Lady John Manners.
  - In the midst of summer there is a lovely display of delphiniums; 30-40 varieties of blues, purples and whites.
  - Yew topiary in the garden of the adjoining cottage portray a boar's head and a peacock-crests of the Vernon and Manners families
  - Note: The feeling is warm and very romantic. Romeo, Romeo!

CHATSWORTH
- Hours of Admission: 11:00 to 4:30
- Location: 2 miles south of Baslow on B6012
- Experience five centuries of British garden history.
- This fabulous manor, set in the wooded valley on River Derwent, has been the home of the Cavendish family for 450 years.
- The original house was built in 1555. It was remodeled between 1686 and 1707, extensive alterations were made in the 1820's and the north wing was added in the late 19th century.
- George London and Henry Wise created the grandiose 17th century formal gardens.
- 'Capability' Brown was engaged in 1760 to landscape the 1000 acre park and to sweep away many of the formal features in favor of the 'naturalistic' style of the day.
- Brown created a huge expanse of lawn, Salisbury Lawns, from a series of formal terraces. I've been told this area is large enough to hold three golf holes.
- Joseph Paxton was hired in 1826 as head gardener and during the next thirty years he was responsible for many wonderful alterations and additions.
- Paxton's Conservative Wall, built in 1848, is a unique series of conservatories, 331 feet long in ascending steps. This extraordinary structure is filled with a large collection of tender plants.
- A truly wondrous sight, The Cascade was originally built in 1696. Enjoy the view from the ornamental pavilion that looks out to the glorious countryside and down on fountains and pools and water tumbling over twenty-four groups of stone steps. Another sight to enjoy is adults and children alike splashing through the water.
- Near Flora's Temple you will find a fabulous double sided border. The planting is unique and very well done; July brings bright yellows, reds and oranges. The border across the Broad Walk is quite a contrast in blues and whites.
- Canal Pond dug in 1702 and enlarged in 1843 was renamed the Emporer Fountain after Czar Nicholas. A lovely spot to stop for a little picnic or just a rest.
- You will also find a fabulous display of lupine in spring, a charming rose garden, hundreds of lilies blooming in August, a maze to get lost in, an unusual serpentine beech hedge, a grotto and much more.
- Note: This is a big place, expect to do a lot of walking. It is a long, lovely road that leads to the manor. Watch out for the sheep and be sure to stop for a couple pictures- great views of the house! Very popular.

OTHER GARDENS IN THE AREA: HARDWICK HALL, CLUMBER PARK

The Pavillion looks down on the fabulous Cascade at Chatsworth.

RENISHAW HALL
- Hours of Admission: 10:30 to 4:30
- Location: 6 miles equidistant from Sheffield & Chesterfield on A616
- A lovely surprise! Situated in the foothill of the Pennines overlooking Rother Valley, we found seven acres of formal gardens surrounded by three hundred acres of parkland.
- The first Renishaw Hall was built in 1625 but the Sitwell family has lived on these grounds since the 14th century.
- The gardens you see today were designed by Sir George Sitwell beginning in the late 19th century. He was a passionate gardener with a great love for the gardens of the Italian Renaissance. He made several trips to Italy and visited over two hundred gardens.
- His friend, Sir Edwin Lutyens influenced Sir George in his design. In 1910 Gertrude Jekyll was asked for a planting scheme, unfortunately she suggested several bright flowering plants which Sir George hated and she was not asked again.
- The garden is designed in a series of descending terraces, linked by stone steps. The symmetry of the design provides lovely views and vistas.
- Low boxwood and higher yew hedges create a series of garden rooms. One room is edged by rambling roses and contains several tall rectangular yew topiaries.
- As you might expect several Italian statues enhance the garden. One of these is Diana and Neptune. Diana is quite charming, she has her dog seated next to her.
- In one area a magnificent oak, planted in 1815 to commemorate the Battle of Waterloo, provides a wonderful canopy.
- One of my favorite features, the charming stone Gothick Temple, now in ruins, was once an aviary.
- Note: I was very impressed with this little known garden. All the shapes, forms, terraces and countryside views provide many photo opportunities. Check out the golf course near by, if you have time to play a round.

TOUR #9
MAP

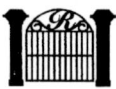

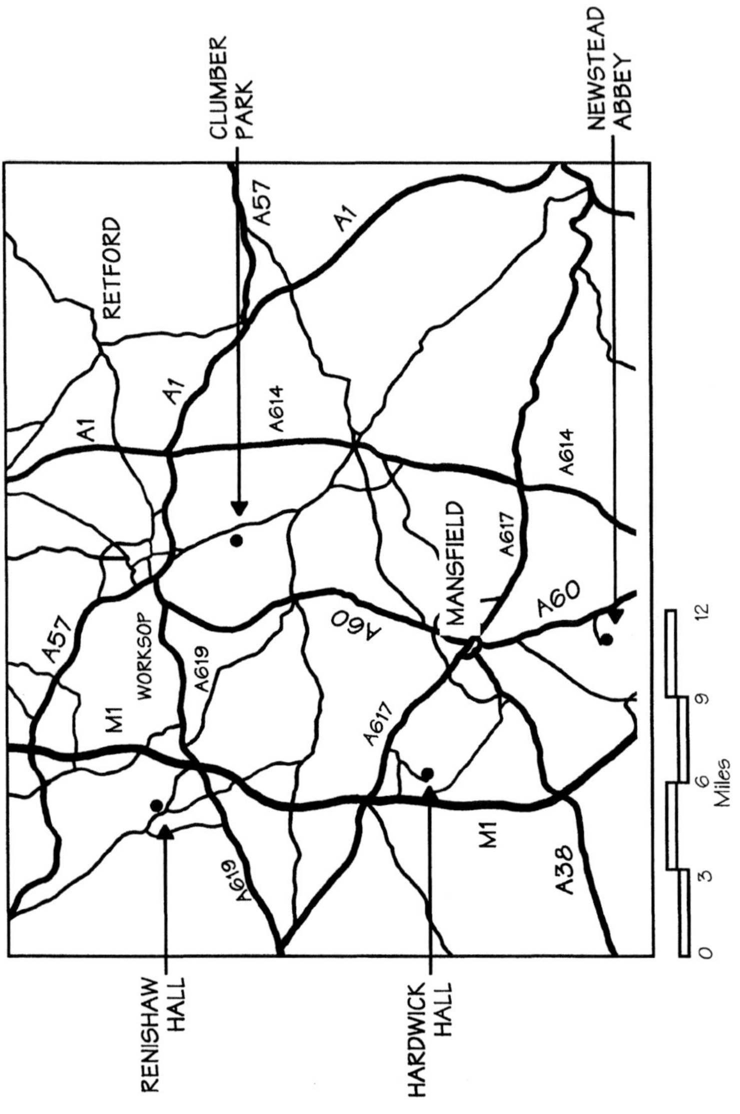
CLUMBER PARK
NEWSTEAD ABBEY
RETFORD
A57
A1
A1
A1
A614
A614
WORKSOP
A57
M1
A619
A60
A60
MANSFIELD
A617
A617
A619
M1
A38
RENISHAW HALL
HARDWICK HALL
0
3
6
9
12
Miles

TOUR #9

* HARDWICK HALL
* NEWSTEAD ABBEY
* RENISHAW HALL

• FRIDAY, SATURDAY, SUNDAY •

It is often wise to allow enough time to visit both the garden and the house. Such is the case at Hardwick Hall. The beauty of both come together and provide a real feel for this 16th century estate. Renishaw Hall will inspire many photo opportunities with all its shapes, colors and country views. The third stop will be the lovely 20th century gardens at the 12th century Newstead Abbey. You will need up to two hours at each of these three gardens. Travel time between Newstead and Hardwick is 20 minutes. Travel time between Hardwick and Renishaw is 20 minutes.

HARDWICK HALL (N.T.)
- Hours of Admission: 12:00 to 5:30
- Location: 9.5 miles southeast of Chesterfield
    - This seven acre estate was built as a hunting lodge in 16th century. It is unfortunate that only walls & gazebos remain from late 16th century garden.
    - Allees of yew and hornbeam divide the garden into quadrants. One quarter is a large expanse of lawn with Hungarian oaks, borders of roses and herbaceous plants; two quarters are orchards with twisted old apple trees, glorious wildflower lawn & fragrant shrub roses; the other quarter is a modern orchard with old varieties that provide an abundance of color in the spring.
    - Elizabethan herb garden (200x100 feet) was laid out in the old vegetable garden in the 1970s. Clipped yew hedges surround colorful mixed beds with the veggies, a large potato patch, herbs and big standards of hops throughout. A great mix.
    - Take time to visit the house. You will find glorious tapestries and a very interesting collection of portraits that define several centuries of history. Don't forget to ask about the traditional floor covering in the great rooms on the upper floor.
    - Note: Repair work done to ornamentation on top of the walls is in the excellent National Trust tradition. Hope you don't have to confront too many cows on the way in. I laughed so hard!

At Newstead Abbey lovely flower beds are bordered by box hedges.

NEWSTEAD ABBEY
- Hours of Admission: 9:00 to 6:00
- Location: 12 miles north of Nottingham along A60
  - Founded as a prior between 1163 and 1173, this was the historic home of poet, Lord Byron.
  - Water flows into the beautiful garden lake through an ornamental cascade. An interesting view of the Abbey and garden is from behind the cascade through the 'window' of water.
  - The old walled kitchen garden is now the rose garden, designed in a symmetrical pattern with a fountain and glorious old-fashioned roses.
  - Be adventuresome and wander out from the walled garden. Walk around the lake to the entrance to the Japanese garden.
  - Early 20th century Japanese garden is well designed with stepping stones, humpbacked bridges, Japanese maples and a lovely assortment of lush plants.
  - In early summer a large iris garden is a riot of color. The beds are bordered by boxwood hedges and shaded by old pear trees.
  - Stroll behind the Abbey and you will find flower beds surrounding a large sunken pool. On the terrace level above several large trees decorate a wide expanse of lawn. To one side of the terrace, a colorful mixed border lines the wonderful brick and stone wall which extends 150-200 yards.
  - Another interesting feature is the sunken Spanish garden. The design is formal, an old well is surrounded by boxwood hedges and several small beds of annuals (marigolds in summer).

OTHER GARDENS IN THE AREA: HADDON HALL, CHATSWORTH, CLUMBER PARK

RENISHAW HALL

- Hours of Admission: 10:30 to 4:30
- Location: 6 miles equidistant from Sheffield & Chesterfield on A616
- A lovely surprise! Situated in the foothill of the Pennines overlooking Rother Valley, we found seven acres of formal gardens surrounded by three hundred acres of parkland.
- The first Renishaw Hall was built in 1625 but the Sitwell family has lived on these grounds since the 14th century.
- The gardens you see today were designed by Sir George Sitwell beginning in the late 19th century. He was a passionate gardener with a great love for the gardens of the Italian Renaissance. He made several trips to Italy and visited over two hundred gardens.
- His friend, Sir Edwin Lutyens influenced Sir George in his design. In 1910 Gertrude Jekyll was asked for a planting scheme, unfortunately she suggested several bright flowering plants which Sir George hated and she was not asked again.
- The garden is designed in a series of descending terraces, linked by stone steps. The symmetry of the design provides lovely views and vistas.
- Low boxwood and higher yew hedges create a series of garden rooms. One room is edged by rambling roses and contains several tall rectangular yew topiaries.
- As you might expect several Italian statues enhance the garden. One of these is Diana and Neptune. Diana is quite charming, she has her dog seated next to her.
- In one area a magnificent oak, planted in 1815 to commemorate the Battle of Waterloo, provides a wonderful canopy.
- One of my favorite features, the charming stone Gothick Temple, now in ruins, was once an aviary.
- For many years the most northern vineyard in Western Europe existed at Renishaw.
- Note: I was very impressed with this little known garden. All the shapes, forms, terraces and countryside views provide many photo opportunities. Check out the golf course near by, if you have time for a round.

The romantic Gothick Temple at Renishaw.

TOUR #10
MAP

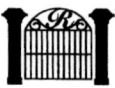

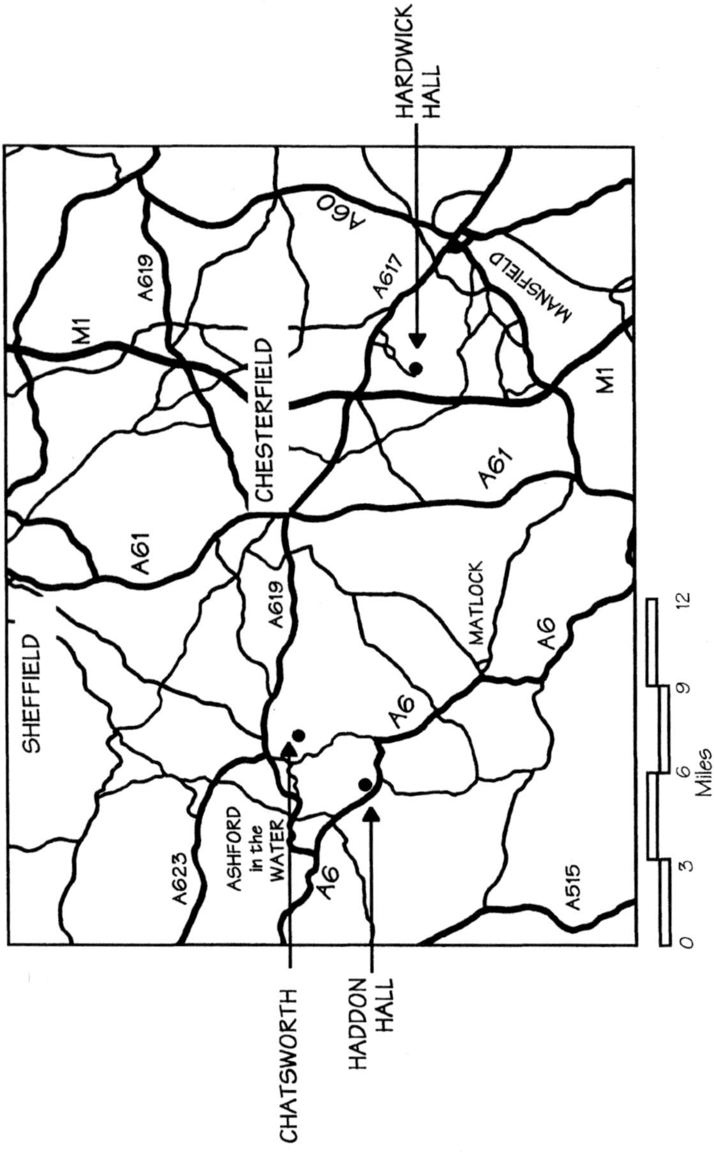

HARDWICK HALL
A60
A617
MANSFIELD
A619
M1
CHESTERFIELD
M1
A61
A61
MATLOCK
A619
A6
SHEFFIELD
A6
ASHFORD in the WATER
A623
A6
A515
CHATSWORTH
HADDON HALL
0 3 6 9 12
Miles

TOUR #10

* CHATSWORTH
* HADDON HALL
* HARDWICK HALL

• MONDAY THROUGH THURSDAY •

The grandeur of a landscape touched by five centuries of British history and many great designers awaits you at Chatsworth. Take your time, plan on at least three hours. Roses are a specialty at the romantic Haddon Hall. Stone terraces and walls provide the backdrop for glorious color and sweet fragrance of hundreds of roses. If you love roses like I do, at least two hours are needed here. A good place to start the day is at Hardwick Hall, a lovely garden restored in this century. An hour or two is needed here. Travel time between Hardwick and Chatsworth is 25 minutes. Travel time between Chatsworth and Haddon is 10 minutes.

HARDWICK HALL (N.T.)
- Hours of Admission: 12:00 to 5:30
- Location: 9.5 miles southeast of Chesterfield
  - This seven acre estate was built as a hunting lodge in 16th century. Unfortunately only walls & gazebos remain from late 16th century garden.
  - Allees of yew and hornbeam divide the garden into quadrants. One quarter is a large expanse of lawn with Hungarian oaks, borders of roses and herbaceous plants; two quarters are orchards with twisted old apple trees, glorious wildflower lawn & fragrant shrub roses; the other quarter is a modern orchard with old varieties that provide an abundance of color in the spring.
  - Elizabethan herb garden (200x100 feet) was laid out in the old vegetable garden in the 1970s. Clipped yew hedges surround colorful mixed beds with the veggies, a large potato patch, herbs and big standards of hops throughout. A great mix.
  - Take time to visit the house. You will find glorious tapestries and a very interesting collection of portraits that define several centuries of history. Don't forget to ask about the traditional floor covering in the great rooms on the upper floor.
  - Note: Repair work done to ornamentation on top of the walls is in the excellent National Trust tradition.

Chatsworth

CHATSWORTH
- Hours of Admission: 11:00 to 4:30
- Location: 2 miles south of Baslow on B6012
- Experience five centuries of British garden history.
- This fabulous manor, set in the wooded valley on River Derwent, has been the home of the Cavendish family for 450 years.
- The original house was built in 1555. It was remodeled between 1686 and 1707, extensive alterations were made in the 1820's and the north wing was added in the late 19th century.
- George London and Henry Wise created the grandiose 17th century formal gardens.
- 'Capability' Brown was engaged in 1760 to landscape the 1000 acre park and to sweep away many of the formal features in favor of the 'naturalistic' style of the day.
- Brown created a huge expanse of lawn, Salisbury Lawns, from a series of formal terraces. I've been told this area is large enough to hold three golf holes.
- Joseph Paxton was hired in 1826 as head gardener and during the next thirty years he was responsible for many wonderful alterations and additions.
- Paxton's Conservative Wall, built in 1848, is a unique series of conservatories, 331 feet long in ascending steps. This extraordinary structure is filled with a large collection of tender plants.
- A truly wondrous sight, The Cascade was originally built in 1696. Enjoy the view from the ornamental pavilion that looks out to the glorious countryside and down on fountains and pools and water tumbling over twenty-four groups of stone steps. Another sight to enjoy is adults and children alike splashing through the water.
- Near Flora's Temple you will find a fabulous double sided border. The planting is unique and very well done; July brings bright yellows, reds and oranges. The border across the Broad Walk is quite a contrast in blues and whites.
- Canal Pond dug in 1702 and enlarged in 1843 was renamed the Emporer Fountain after Czar Nicholas. A lovely spot to stop for a little picnic or just a rest.
- You will also find a fabulous display of lupine in spring, a charming rose garden, hundreds of lilies blooming in August, a maze to get lost in, an unusual serpentine beech hedge, a grotto and much more.
- Note: This is a big place, expect to do a lot of walking. It is a long, lovely road that leads to the manor. Watch out for the sheep and be sure to stop for a couple pictures- great views of the house! Very popular.

HADDON HALL
- Hours of Admission: 11:00 to 5:45
- Location: 2.5 miles southeast of Bakewell on A6
  - What you see today is the most complete surviving medieval manor house in England. Haddon Hall has been on this site since before the Domesday survey in 1087. Sited on an outcrop overlooking the River Wye, it has been the home of Manners and Vernon families since 12th century.
  - The garden is entered through a portion of the house and down a flight of worn stone steps constructed in 1649.
  - Although there are records of the garden dating back to the late 16th century, the present garden dates back to the early 18th century. In the early 20th century a massive clearance and replanting was needed in this horribly overgrown garden.
  - The terraced rose garden has been created from stones quarried locally (Cotswold stone look). The walls drop down 18-24 feet to the River Wye below. Look down and you will find a lovely waterfall.
  - Roses are definitely a specialty! Castle walls, balustrades edging the terraces and staircases make perfect places for climbing roses intermingled with clematis. You will find over 150 varieties of roses including many that are seventy years old. What a fabulous riot of color and fragrance!
  - Look for a very special rose, 'Mary Manners', named after Lady John Manners.
  - In the midst of summer there is a lovely display of delphiniums; 30-40 varieties of blues, purples and whites.
  - Yew topiary in the garden of the adjoining cottage portray a boar's head and a peacock-crests of the Vernon and Manners families
  - Note: The feeling is warm and very romantic. Romeo, Romeo!

Romantic Haddon Hall.

OTHER GARDENS IN THE AREA: RENISHAW HALL, NEWSTEAD ABBEY, CLUMBER PARK

TOUR #11
MAP

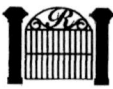

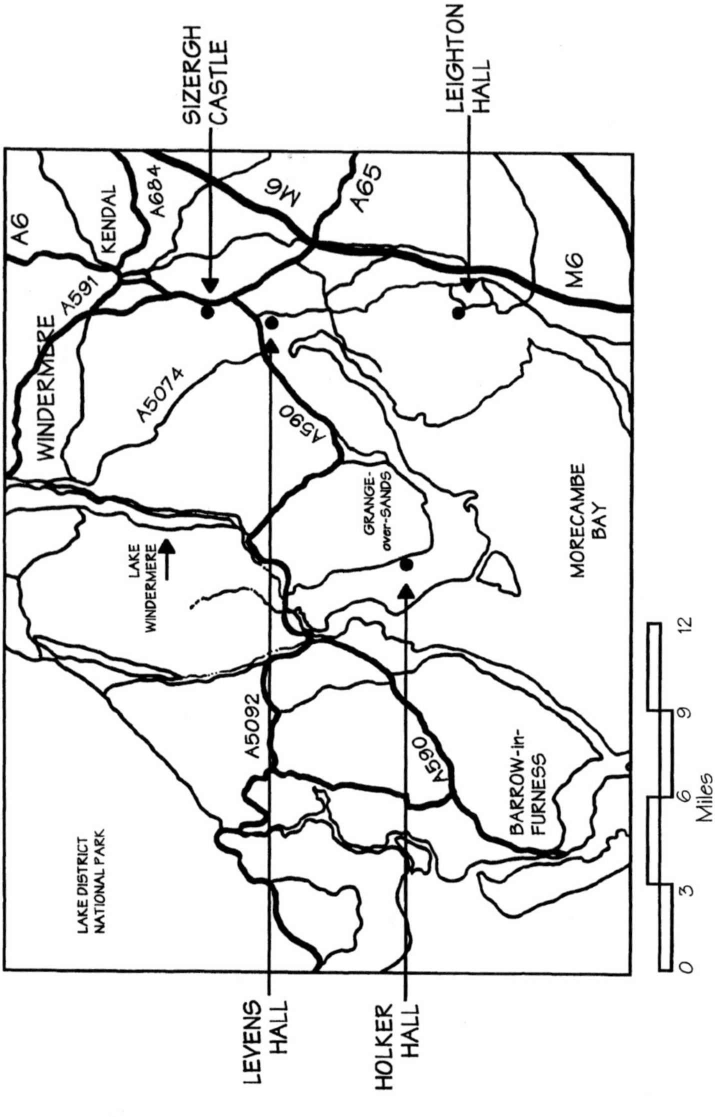

SIZERGH CASTLE
LEIGHTON HALL
LEVENS HALL
HOLKER HALL
KENDAL
A6
A684
A65
M6
M6
A591
WINDERMERE
A5074
A590
A590
A5092
GRANGE-over-SANDS
LAKE WINDERMERE
MORECAMBE BAY
BARROW-in-FURNESS
LAKE DISTRICT NATIONAL PARK
0
3
6
9
12
Miles

TOUR #11
* SIZERGH CASTLE
* LEVENS HALL
* HOLKER HALL

• SUNDAY THROUGH THURSDAY •

Here we are in the southern part of the wonderful Lake District. If you love topiaries, Levens Hall is the place for you. What an amazing collection of shapes and sizes! At least two hours are needed for a thorough inspection. The grand Victorian style mixed with herbaceous borders and the interesting Neptune Cascade are the attractions at Holker Hall. The imposing limestone rock garden at Sizergh Castle may give you some ideas for a smaller one at home. One to two hours each are needed at these two gardens. Travel time between Holker Hall and Levens Hall is 15 minutes. Travel time between Levens and Sizergh Castle is 10 minutes.

SIZERGH CASTLE (N.T.)
- Hours of Admission: 12:30 to 5:30
- Location: 3.5 miles south of Kendal
  - An impressive 14th century Pele Tower forms the core of this castle which was remodeled in the 16th and 17th centuries. It has been home for the Strickland family for over 750 years.
  - The most imposing feature of the garden is a three quarter acre limestone rock garden planted in 1926. The cooler, damper climate is not appropriate for a true alpine garden. Plants suitable for the climate were chosen: Japanese maples, a large selection of dwarf conifers and a superb collection of ferns (part of the National Collection of Hardy Ferns). The largest rock garden owned by the National Trust.
  - You will also enjoy a one hundred yard fuchsia walk, colorful herbaceous borders, a fragrant rose garden and the vibrant color from springs bulbs and autumn foliage.

At Holker Hall see Victorian in its grandest scale.

LEVENS HALL
- Hours of Admission: 11:00 to 5:00
- Location: 5 miles south of Kendal on A6
- "best, oldest and most extensive topiary garden in the world"
- The Elizabethan stone mansion you see today dates back about 300 years but the original Pele Tower and hall date from between 1250 and 1300. It was purchased or 'won' by Colonel James Grahme in 1688. It was the Colonel who hired Guillaume Beaumont.
- This world famous topiary garden was first laid out in 1694 and has largely remained unaltered. The only existing example of Beaumont's work, it remains intact because the family refused to give in to the 'naturalistic' style of the 18th century.
- Topiary Town, an amazing assortment of shapes, sizes and forms clipped from boxwood and yew in many colors including golden yew that really stand out against all the green. There are ninety topiaries in all, some of the trees and bushes are 300 years old. The formal shapes are framed by the underplanting of colorful flowers.
- Topiaries are clipped once a year in late August and September and it takes 4-6 weeks with electrical clippers. Think how long it must have taken with hand shears.
- The rose parterre was laid out in the 1950's but was replanted recently with David Austin roses which gives old rose color, scent and flower form but also gives a repeating bloom; again underplanted with soft colored perennials.
- 15,000 plants are used as bedding plants in the parterres and are changed twice a year. Fabulous color and good foliage contrasts are highlights of these parterres.
- Fabulous beech rondel with great beech allees leading off in two directions and wide double borders filled with roses and perennials radiating out in two directions. It takes two people six weeks to clip these beeches.
- The main park, a part of Beaumont's original design, is now across the road. Here you will find an oak avenue that extends for over a mile and runs parallel to the River Kent.
- Note: We decided that its like walking in *Alice in Wonderland* with all the funny shapes and sizes.

Magical topiaries at Levens Hall.

At Holker Hall the Statue of Neptune stands proudly at the top of his Cascade.

HOLKER HALL

- Hours of Admission: 10:00 to 6:00
- Location: 4 miles southwest of Grange-over-Sands on B5277
  - Even though the original house was built in the 16th century, what you see today is Victorian in its grandest scale.
- The formal early 18th century gardens were swept away in favor of a 'natural' parkland in the later part of that century.
- Once again in the 19th century, formal gardens were created and mixed with a lovely woodland garden.
- The woodland garden was first laid out in the mid-19th century by Joseph Paxton. Mild climate and acid soils are ideal for terrific old trees that provide a canopy for thousands of bulbs, wildflowers, glorious rhododendrons and azaleas (some rhododendrons are 100 years old) and an Italian fountain.
- Mixed borders of herbaceous plants in soft pinks and blues, old fashioned roses and peonies surrounded by clipped hornbeam and beech hedges and big pots overflowing with color create wonderful formal gardens.
- Enjoy Neptune Cascade. Water flows over a series of limestone steps on several levels to a lovely pond and fountain below. Gravity provides the power for this interesting feature.
- Charming sunken rose garden, backed by a stone wall and vine covered garden house, has been restored to its early 20th century design.
- You will also find a cedar of Lebanon that survives from the late 18th century and one hundred and twenty-five acres of deer park.
- Note: A good example of how young yew are planted to create hedges over many years. The lady of the house must love blues and pinks.

OTHER GARDENS IN THE AREA: LEIGHTON HALL, BRANTWOOD, HOLEHIRD GARDENS, RYDAL MOUNT

TOUR #12

MAP

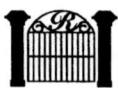

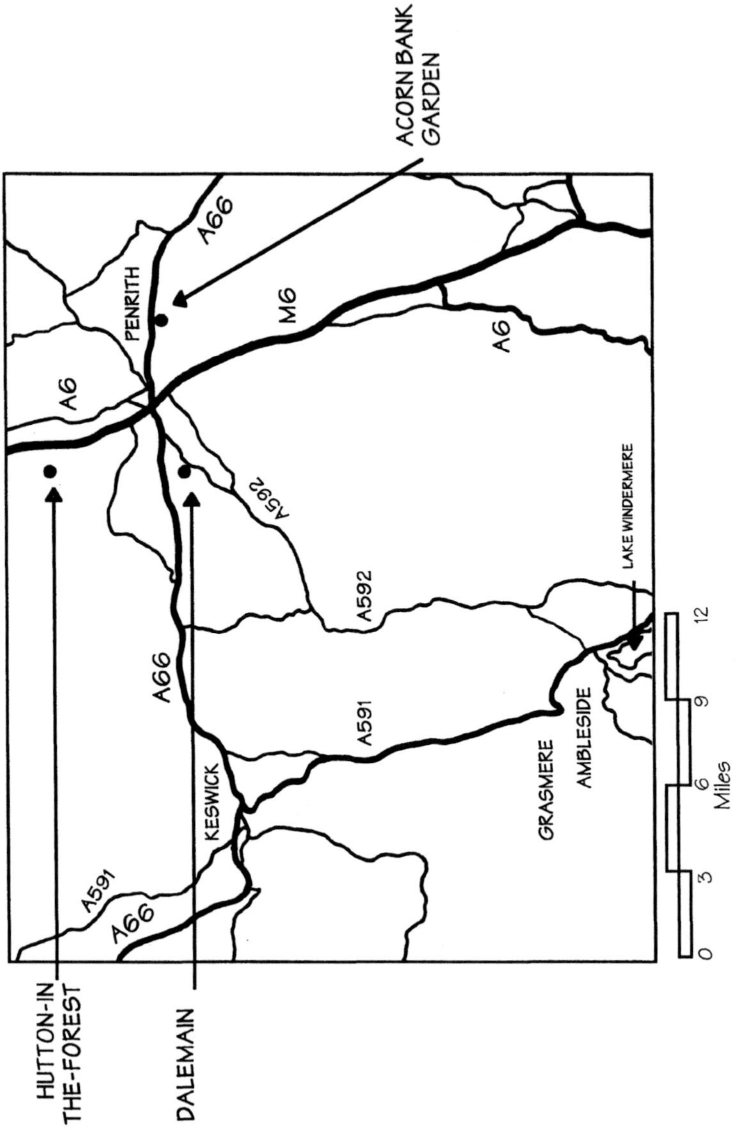
ACORN BANK GARDEN
PENRITH
A66
M6
A6
A6
A592
A592
LAKE WINDERMERE
A66
A591
KESWICK
GRASMERE
AMBLESIDE
A591
A66
0 3 6 9 12
Miles
HUTTON-IN THE-FOREST
DALEMAIN

Garden Tours of England

TOUR #12
* ACORN BANK GARDEN
* DALEMAIN
* HUTTON-IN-THE-FOREST

• DAILY EXCEPT FRIDAY & SATURDAY •

You may want to take one of the winding country roads to the northern Lake District around Penrith. Here you will find three rather different gardens. The Tudor Knot Garden and blue poppies mixed with old-fashioned roses bordering a long walk are the highlights at Dalemain. A medieval forest at Hutton-in-the-Forest surrounds charming topiary terraces and a large colorful walled garden. The third stop is at Acorn Bank, a great place to study culinary and medicinal plants. One to two hours are needed at each garden. Travel time between Dalmain and Hutton is 15 minutes. Travel time between Hutton and Acorn Bank is 15 minutes.

ACORN BANK GARDEN (N.T.)
- Hours of Admission: 10:00 to 5:30
- Location: 6 miles east of Penrith on A66
  - Protected by fine oaks, this two and a half acre garden displays a vast array of daffodils, tulips and anemones in spring.
  - Inside garden walls you will find two orchards surrounded by mixed borders; colorful herbaceous plants and roses mix happily with fruit trees.
  - Housed in the old walled vegetable garden, the impressive 45x22 foot physic or herb garden has the largest collection of culinary and medicinal plants (250 varieties of herbs) in the north. A fine peony border greets you at the entrance and on a warm summer day the fragrance of herbs fill the air.
  - Note: The house is not open to the public.

One of the lovely sculptures you will find at Dalemain.

DALEMAIN

- Hours of Admission: 11:15 to 5:00
- Location: southwest of Penrith on A592
  - The manor is a fine mixture of Tudor, Medieval and Georgian architecture. The impressive Georgian facade is complimented by a cobbled courtyard. The family has lived here since 1679.
  - The gardens also have a long and varied history stretching back to a medieval herb garden.
  - One of the finest features of the garden is the Tudor Knott Garden. A lovely early Roman fountain is surrounded by box-edged beds filled with tulips, herbs and violas.
  - Along the Rose Walk you will find over one hundred fragrant old fashioned roses and a collection of ancient apple trees underplanted with the soft colors of herbaceous plants including blue Himalayon Poppies.
  - Look for the largest silver fir tree in the United Kingdom; 85 feet high and a girth of 19 feet.
  - Note: Enjoy tea and homemade pastries in the medieval hall which dates back to 1400. A charming garden but maintenance could be better.

Stone steps lead you to sunken beds at Acorn Bank.

Charming Tudor Knot Garden surrounds Roman fountain in Dalemain.

HUTTON-IN-THE-FOREST

- Hours of Admission: 11:00 to 5:00
- Location: 7 miles northwest of Penrith on B5305
  - Built around a medieval Pele Tower, the manor has had several additions in several styles over the centuries. See if you can figure out which is the oldest portion.
  - As the name implies, Hutton is surrounded by the woodland of the medieval Forest of Inglewood.
  - Charming topiary terraces, dated from 17th century, are filled with roses, rhododendrons and giant clipped yews.
  - A large walled garden is designed in a series of rooms. You will find lovely herbaceous borders in soft blues, pinks, purples and yellows, a dovecote and fountains of pink 'Fairy' roses. Check out the size of the trunks on the espaliered apples.
  - Enjoy a walk through the pleasure grounds down to a lovely five acre ornamental lake.

OTHER GARDENS IN THE AREA: RYDAL MOUNT, DOVE COTTAGE

TOUR #13

MAP

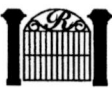

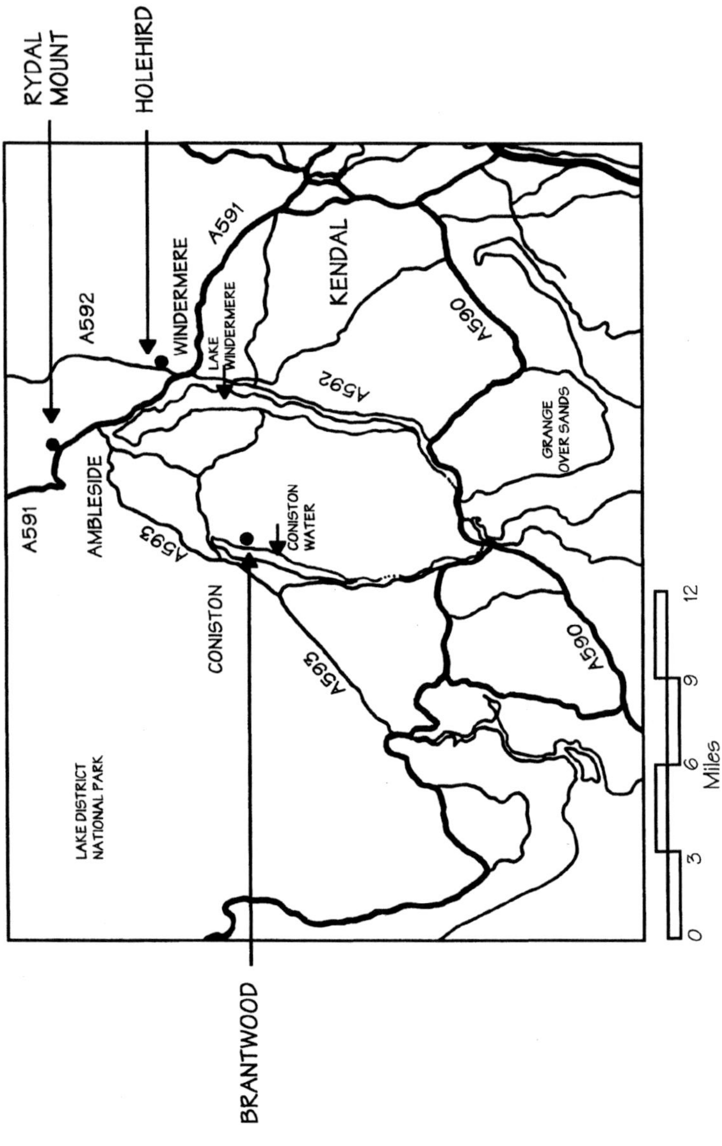

RYDAL MOUNT
HOLEHIRD
WINDERMERE
A591
A592
KENDAL
LAKE WINDERMERE
A590
A592
GRANGE OVER SANDS
A591
AMBLESIDE
A593
CONISTON WATER
CONISTON
A593
A590
LAKE DISTRICT NATIONAL PARK
BRANTWOOD
0
3
6
9
12
Miles

# TOUR #13

* BRANTWOOD
* RYDAL MOUNT
* HOLEHIRD

• DAILY •

Right in the heart of the Lake District with bustling towns, imposing mountains and the blue waters of lovely lakes you can enjoy four charming gardens. Beautiful borders and glorious views of the countryside are yours to behold at Holehird. This botanical garden can provide many good ideas for your own garden. One to two hours are needed here. For something a little different, pick up the Gondola Boat at Coniston and cruise to the gardens at Brantwood. Plan on about two hours if you take the cruise. Between Ambleside and Grasmere visit two lovely gardens, the homes of William Wordsworth, Rydal Mount and Dove Cottage. Up to an hour is needed at each of these two gardens. Travel time between Holehird and Rydal Mount is 15 minutes. Travel time between Rydal Mount and Dove is 25 minutes. Travel time between Dove and Brantwood is 20 minutes.

BRANTWOOD
- Hours of Admission: 11:00 to 5:30
- Location: south of Coniston
  - The home of social revolutionary, John Ruskin from 1872 to 1900, this was one of the foremost literary and artistic centers in Europe.
  - From the terrace surrounding the house enjoy the finest lake and mountain views in England.
  - Thirty acres of gardens extend from the lake up the hill behind the house.
  - Primarily a woodland garden that is especially lovely in spring when azaleas form a frame around the house and in fall when autumn color surrounds it.
  - Note: You can drive but this is a great opportunity to take the Steam Yacht 'Gondola' from Coniston right to Brantwood.

Steam Yacht 'Gondola'

Fell-side terraces below the house at Rydal Mount.

RYDAL MOUNT
- Hours of Admission: 9:30 to 5:00
- Location: 1.5 miles from Ambleside on A591
  - The historic home of William Wordsworth from 1813 until his death in 1850.
  - Four and a half acres of glorious gardens were created by the poet.
  - A charming summerhouse overlooks Rydal Water and provides glorious views.
  - Acid soils and cooler temperatures provide the perfect environment for daffodils, bluebells, rhododendrons and azaleas that provide a spectacular display of color in spring.
  - You will also find fell side terraces, rare shrubs and a nice collection of heaths and heathers.
  - Note: Parking can be difficult.

DOVE COTTAGE
- Hours of Admission: 9:30 to 5:30
- Location: 2.5 miles fron Ambleside on A591
  - William Wordsworth home in the early years from 1799-1808.
  - Be sure to visit the museum, it diplays the Wordsworth Trust collection of manuscripts, books and paintings.
  - You will find a simple cottage garden with views directly over Grasmere and onto the fells.
  - Note: You might want to inquire about one of the six lovely rooms in the guest house.

HOLEHIRD

- Hours of Admission: 9:00 to 6:00
- Location: on A592, 1 mile north of junction with A591
  - A fabulous botanical garden in the heart of the Lake District. This three and a half acre hillside garden overlooks the Troutbeck Valley.
  - A wonderful collection of planting beds are contained within old brick walls.
  - A good place to study design, the plants in each bed are selected for color, size and foliage contrast. Each plant is well labeled.
  - National Collection of astilbes and hydrangeas provide a wonderful display.
  - You can also enjoy glorious views of the countryside.
  - Note: I was very impressed. It was even lovely in the rain. All work is done by volunteers and there are always nice people around to answer questions and chat.

Walk along this path and enjoy the colorful
National Collection of astilbes at Holehird.

OTHER GARDENS IN THE AREA: SIZERGH CASTLE, LEVENS HALL, HOLKER HALL

TOUR #14

MAP

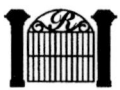

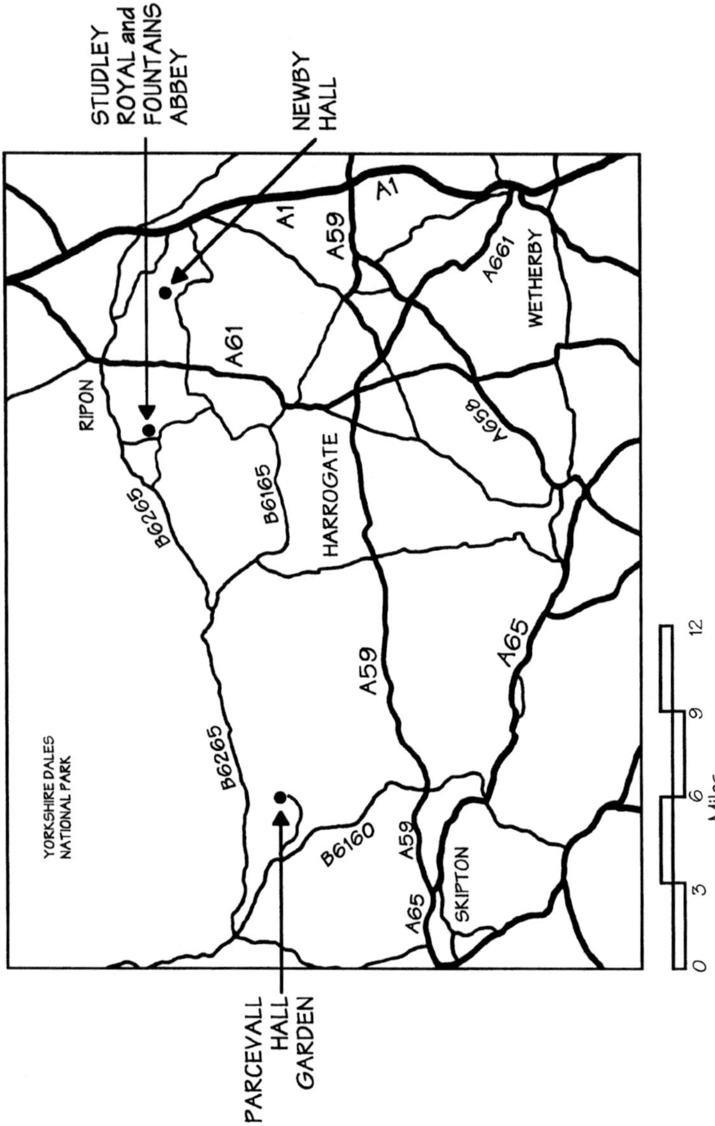

STUDLEY ROYAL and FOUNTAINS ABBEY
NEWBY HALL
PARCEVALL HALL GARDEN
A1
A59
A61
A661
A658
A65
B6265
B6165
B6160
RIPON
HARROGATE
WETHERBY
SKIPTON
YORKSHIRE DALES NATIONAL PARK
0
3
6
9
12
Miles

TOUR #14
* STUDLEY ROYAL & FOUNTAINS ABBEY
* PARCEVALL HALL GARDEN
* NEWBY HALL

• DAILY EXCEPT MONDAY •

The beautiful trip between the Lake District and York is made even better with a visit to Parcevall Hall Garden. Stone terraces, colorful borders, lily ponds and wonderful views of the countryside make this garden worth finding. The fabulous water garden at Studley Royal is made even more imposing by the ruins at Fountains Abbey. I fell in love with the glorious double borders, charming sculpture and beautiful garden rooms at Newby Hall. This has become a new favorite! At least two hours are needed at each garden. Travel time between Parcevall Hall and Studley Royal is one hour. Travel time between Studley and Newby Hall is 20 minutes.

STUDLEY ROYAL and FOUNTAINS ABBEY(N.T.)
- Hours of Admission: 10:00 to 7:00
- Location: 4 miles west of Ripon off B6265
  - Studley Royal is a superb one hundred and fifty acre water garden created between 1716 and 1781 by John Aislabie and his son William. It bridges the gap between two periods of garden style, 17th century formality and the romanticism of the picturesque movement.
  - It is laid out in the flat bottom of a secluded valley and is the least altered Georgian 'green' garden in England.
  - The phenomenal ruins of Fountains Abbey were included into the garden in 1768 when William succeeded in purchasing the Abbey and Fountains Hall. These dark and ominous ruins are the most complete remains of a Cistercian Abbey in the country. The abbey was originally founded in 1132.
  - Water flows down the valley from the Abbey along the canal over cascades into the lake in the park.
  - Yew hedges border the lawn and walkways and frame views of several follies that are reflected in the water. Look for Temple of Fame (1781), Temple of Piety (1740), Banqueting House and Octagon Tower (1738).
  - The National Trust acquired the property in 1983 and began a long-term program of restoration.
  - Note: Expect to do a lot of walking, some up and down. The ruins are very interesting. Studley is a tremendous architectural feat but does not appeal to all.

Ominous ruins at Fountains Abbey.

PARCEVALL HALL GARDEN

- Hours of Admission: 10:00 to 6:00
- Location: 9 miles north of Skipton; 7 miles off A59 at Bolton Abbey
- A wonderful surprise in the middle of nowhere! Parcevall is an excellent example of a terraced garden with incredible views of the countryside.
- Stone house dates back to mid 16th century. Although the buildings had fallen into a bad state of repair, Sir William Milner restored and enlarged the house after he purchased the property in 1927.
- The terraced garden is built below the house on a south facing hillside.
- Top terrace contains mixed borders planted in pastel shades and a lovely round lily pond with a wonderful figure of a woman in the center. The renovated pergola is planted with roses and wisteria.
- On one side of the second terrace you will see a lily pond shaded by a colorful cherry tree and lovely magnolias blooming in late spring.
- On the third terrace you will find a central alcove with shades of blue and pink in the borders. The alcove provides a place to escape the rain or just sit and enjoy the fabulous views of the countryside.
- An interesting rock garden contains a variety of plants including wild azaleas brought from Mt. Krishima in Japan by E.H. Wilson.
- Spring brings thousands of daffodils and narcissus that have naturalized and provide a fabulous show. You will also see several varieties of rhododendrons including many imported from China and the Himalayas.
- Climbing up the old stone house is an Albertine rose on one side of the door and espalier laburnum on the other.
- Notes: Its a long windy road but don't give up; its worth it. A cozy tea room is a good place to stop for homemade pastries and a little local conversation. Appears to be a local gathering spot.

Walk along the lovely terraces at Parcevall Hall.

NEWBY HALL
- Hours of Admission: 11:00 to 5:30
- Location: 4 miles west of A1 toward Ripon
- This wonderful Queen Anne house was built in 1695. The property was sold to the current family in 1748 when the formal 17th century garden was swept away in favor of a landscape park typical of that period.
- The twenty-five acres of glorious gardens you see today began to take form in 1920 and continued to develop over the next fifty years. The design was influenced by Lawrence Johnston and Hidcote.
- The current owners working within the framework of the earlier design have created new vistas, replanted with their favorite plants and added rare and unusual trees and shrubs.
- A charming marble sculpture adorns the center of the lily pond just outside the south entry of the house. From here the garden terraces down and radiates out into several rooms.
- From the first terrace the eye follows a fabulous double sided herbaceous border flanked by yew hedges down to the River Ure. Views are to the countryside and back toward the wonderful house. What a sight, approximately 600 feet of borders!
- War of the Roses border edges the path to Sylvia's Garden. Here red and white roses are mixed with peonies and underplanted with purple lavenders. In Sylvia's Garden you will find soft colors and interest through all seasons.
- In the Rose Garden a lovely fountain with soothing water sounds is surrounded by big shrub roses and a hedge of purple leaf beech mixed with holly.
- Again in the Autumn Garden an urn fountain is surrounded by beds filled with late blooming perennials and walls clad with clematis, roses and honeysuckle.
- Take time to explore the Victorian Rock Garden which was designed by Ellen Willmott in the late 19th century.
- Sandstone pillars and cross beams form the structure for the curving laburnum pergola that was originally planted in 1929. This may be the one that started the trend; remember Barnsley House.
- Note: I fell in love! Take a ride on the little train or a cruise on the 'Yoredale'. A good restaurant for lunch.

Newby Hall

OTHER GARDENS IN THE AREA: RIPLEY CASTLE, HARLOW CARR BOTANICAL GARDEN

TOUR #15
MAP

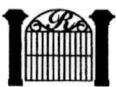

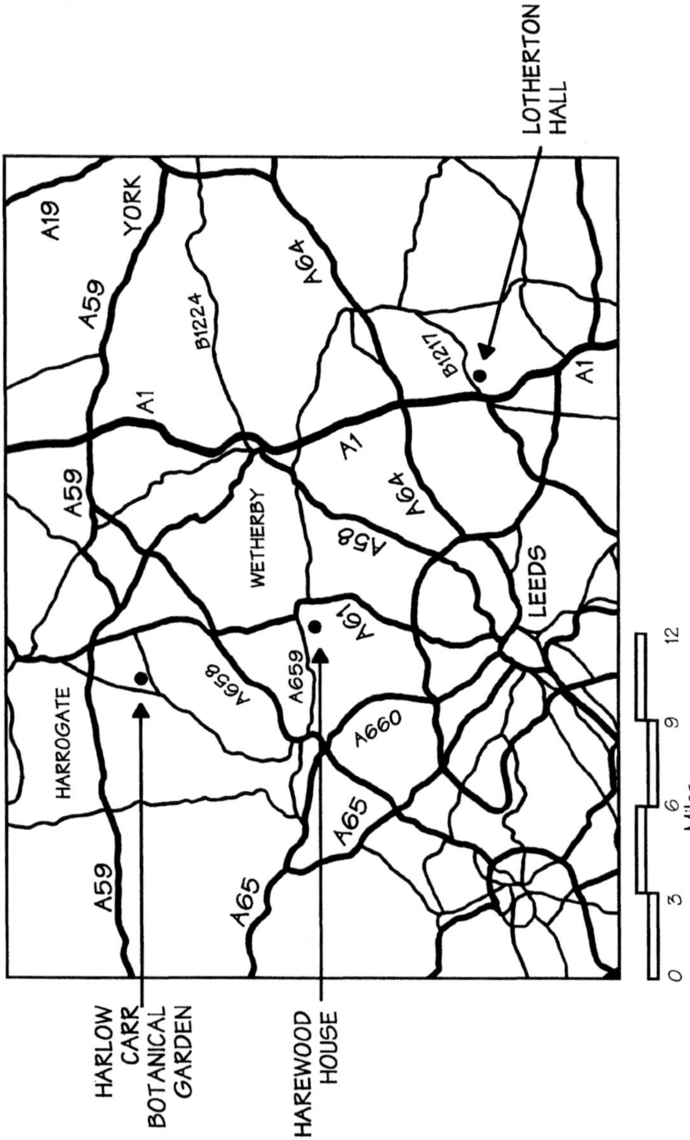
LOTHERTON HALL
YORK
A19
A59
B1224
A64
B1217
A1
WETHERBY
A58
LEEDS
A61
A659
A658
HARROGATE
A660
A65
0
3
6
9
12
Miles
HARLOW CARR BOTANICAL GARDEN
HAREWOOD HOUSE

TOUR #15
* HARLOW CARR BOTANICAL GARDENS
* HAREWOOD HOUSE
* LOTHERTON HALL
• DAILY •

The city of Harrogate is well known for its colorful flower beds and just one and a half miles from the city center Harlow Carr Botanical Garden is no exception. You should find many good ideas. At Harewood House you will be amazed at the recently restored Victorian parterre. What a man, that Orphius! Another fabulous sculpture can be found at Lotherton Hall. The Pilgrim Priest stands proudly in a bed of peonies. You will also find a large enclosed garden filled with fragrant roses. Plan on spending one to two hours at each garden. Travel time between Harlow Carr and Harewood House is 20 minutes. Travel time between Harewood and Lotherton Hall is 40 minutes.

HARLOW CARR BOTANICAL GARDENS
- Hours of Admission: 9:30 to 6:00
- Location: 1.5 miles from Harrogate town center
- With a desire to create 'a Wisley of the North', this sixty-eight acre botanical garden was opened in 1950. It is the headquarters of Northern Horticultural Society.
- The garden was designed and planted for gardeners to provide inspiration and ideas. The plants are well labeled so you'll be able to identify all those items you can't live without.
- As you enter the garden enjoy the formal terrace with sparking waterfall and a riot of color that changes with each season.
- Interesting plant trial beds are used to assess plants for size, uniformity of flowers & susceptibility to pests and disease. During our visit they were testing lobelia and penstemons.
- Limestone rock garden is home for many alpine plants from throughout the world and a lovely collection of Japanese maples. In addition, many ideas for your own garden can be found in the demonstration mini rock gardens.
- You will also find heather, herbaceous borders, a winter garden and woodland garden.
- Note: Carr or car is a boggy area.

Orphius reigns at Harewood Hoise.

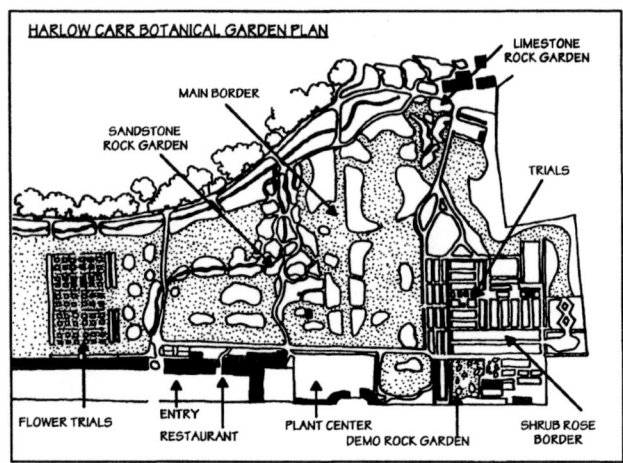

HAREWOOD HOUSE
- Hours of Admission: 10:00 to 6:00
- Location: 8 miles north of Leeds at junction of A659 and A61
  - Completed in 1772, this was the home of the Earl of Harewood for over 200 years. The furniture was made especially for the house by Thomas Chippendale.
- For the nine years, starting in 1772, 'Capability' Brown created the wonderful Parkland setting.
- Humphry Repton added his own ideas in 1800.
- In 1843 Sir Charles Barry, architect of the House of Parliament, added a third story and the massive Terrace and transformed the house from a Georgian country house to an Italian palazzo, both inside and out.
- The Dolphin Garden on the upper terrace has a beautiful sculpture surrounded by lavender beds and a newly planted lime hedge.
- Two of my favorite sculptures, an amazing pair of sphinx guard the house.
- From the balustraded Terrace you view a large parterre with two lovely fountains and a fabulous sculpture of 'Orphius' with a lion draped over his shoulders. The parterre has recently been restored to its original Victorian intricate pattern. It is planted twice a year.
- Enjoy a walk along Harewood Lake. You will find a wonderful collection of rhododendrons and you can wave at the folks cruising by in the wooden launch.
- The four acre Bird Garden is the home to one hundred and twenty species, some of which are considered endangered in their natural habitat. You will also find the infamous pink flamingos.
- Note: Prepare for a lot of walking. A busy spot, weekdays are better. The house contains a fabulous collection of Italian art. Don't venture out to the walled garden, there's nothing there.

LOTHERTON HALL
- Hours of Admission; 10:30 to 6:00
- Location: 3.5 miles northeast of Garforth on B1217
  - A ten acre garden created in the early part of this century is the home to tender plants, rare to this northern area.
  - Terraced area off the house contains lovely colorful rose beds with stone walls surrounding it. Standing in a bed of peonies you will find an outstanding sculpture of a Chinese priest on a bull called 'The Pilgrim Priest'. Read the inscription, the priest loved peonies.
  - Avenue of Victorian pyramidal yews and a simple double sided border leads the eye to a white summerhouse.
  - One of the loveliest features is the long rectangular rose garden enclosed by a tall yew hedge. A herbaceous border along one side and shorter box hedges throughout compliment lovely teas and floribundas which provide quite a fragrance to the garden in high summer.
  - William & Mary sunken garden was laid out in the 17th century in the Dutch style with classical urns and a charming lily pond.
  - Herds of Red and Fallow deer are found in the Deer Park. Its a wonderful place to take a stroll.
  - A large aviary contains a famous collection of two hundred species of rare and endangered birds.
  - Note: A well designed and interesting garden. The house is nothing special.

'The Pilgrim Priest' rests in a bed of peonies.

OTHER GARDENS IN THE AREA: RIPLEY CASTLE

TOUR #16
MAP

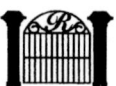

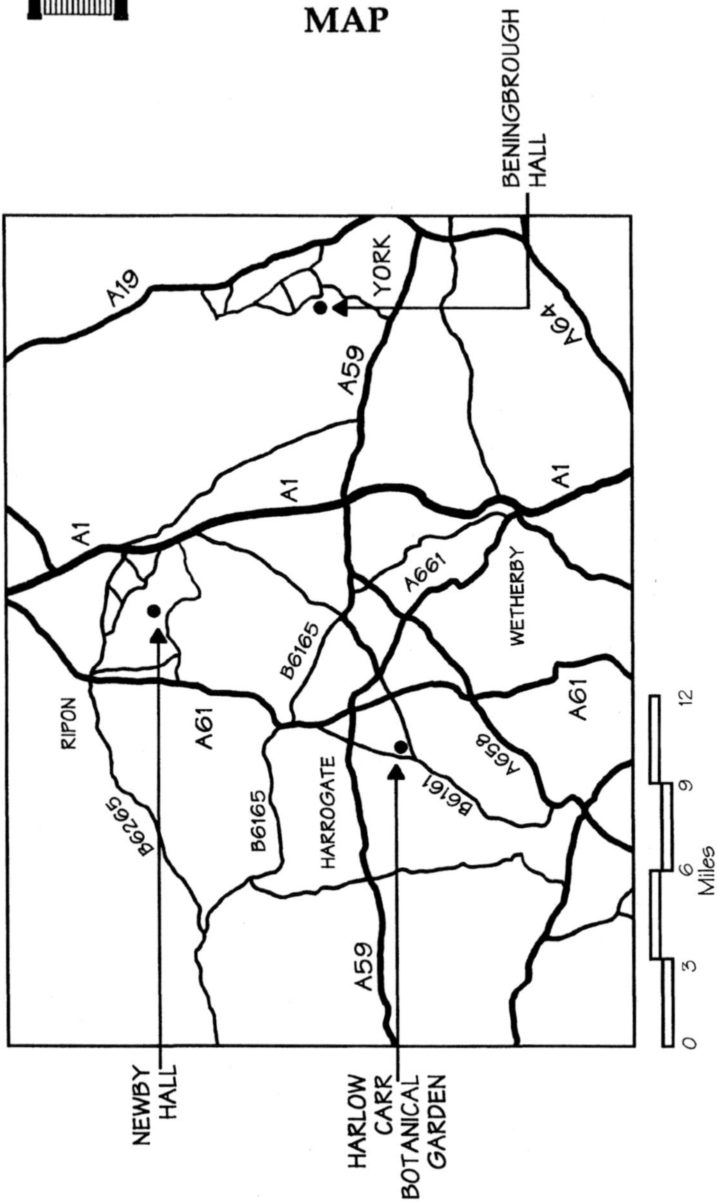
BENINGBROUGH HALL
YORK
A19
A64
A59
A1
A661
WETHERBY
B6165
A61
RIPON
A658
B6161
HARROGATE
B6265
NEWBY HALL
HARLOW CARR BOTANICAL GARDEN
0 3 6 9 12
Miles

TOUR #16
* HARLOW CARR BOTANICAL GARDENS
* NEWBY HALL
* BENINGBROUGH HALL

• SATURDAY, SUNDAY, TUESDAY, WEDNESDAY •

What a sight, a wonderful Queen Anne house and 600 feet of colorful borders! The charming garden rooms at Newby Hall sparkle with color from spring through autumn. Another imposing manor, this time Georgian, can be found at Beningbrough Hall. After you have enjoyed the lovely gardens be sure to take a little extra time to visit the house. At least two hours will be needed to properly enjoy these two gardens. The botanical gardens at Harlow Carr will provide enjoyment and a few good ideas for your own home. Plan on one to two hours. Travel time between Harlow Carr and Newby Hall is 30 minutes. Travel time between Newby Hall and Beningbrough Hall is 40 minutes.

HARLOW CARR BOTANICAL GARDENS
- Hours of Admission: 9:30 to 6:00
- Location: 1.5 miles from Harrogate town center
  - With the desire to create 'a Wisley of the North', this sixty-eight acre botanical garden was first opened in 1950. It is the headquarters of Northern Horticultural Society.
  - The garden was designed and planted for gardeners to provide ideas and inspiration. The plants are well labeled so you'll be able to identify all those items you can't live without.
  - As you enter the garden enjoy the formal terrace with sparking waterfall and a riot of color that changes with each season.
  - Interesting plant trial beds are used to assess plants for size, uniformity of flowers & susceptibility to pests and disease. During our visit they were testing lobelia and penstemons.
  - Limestone rock garden is home for many alpine plants from areas throughout the world and a lovely collection of Japanese maples. In addition visit the demonstration mini rock gardens for good ideas for your own garden.
  - You will also find heather, scented foliage, herbaceous borders, a winter garden, wild flower meadow and woodland garden.
  - Note: Carr or car is a boggy area.

Gardens and a Queen Anne house at Newby Hall.

NEWBY HALL
- Hours of Admission: 11:00 to 5:30
- Location: 4 miles west of A1 toward Ripon
- This wonderful Queen Anne house was built in 1695. The property was sold to the current family in 1748 when the formal 17th century garden was swept away in favor of a landscape park typical of that period.
- The twenty-five acres of glorious gardens you see today began to take form in 1920 and continued to develop over the next fifty years. The design was influenced by Lawrence Johnston and Hidcote.
- The current owners working within the framework of the earlier design have created new vistas, replanted with their favorite plants and added rare and unusual trees and shrubs.
- A charming marble sculpture adorns the center of the lily pond just outside the south entry of the house. From here the garden terraces down and radiates out into several rooms.
- From the first terrace the eye follows a fabulous double sided herbaceous border flanked by yew hedges down to the River Ure. Views are to the countryside and back toward the wonderful house. What a sight, approximately 600 feet of borders!
- War of the Roses border edges the path to Sylvia's Garden. Here red and white roses are mixed with peonies and underplanted with purple lavenders. In Sylvia's Garden you will find soft colors and interest through all seasons.
- In the Rose Garden a lovely fountain with soothing water sounds is surrounded by big shrub roses and a hedge of purple leaf beech mixed with holly.
- Again in the Autumn Garden an urn fountain is surrounded by beds filled with late blooming perennials and walls clad with clematis, roses and honeysuckle.
- Take time to explore the Victorian Rock Garden which was designed by Ellen Willmott in the late 19th century.
- Sandstone pillars and cross beams form the structure for the curving laburnum pergola that was originally planted in 1929. This may be the one that started the trend; remember Barnsley House.
- Note: I fell in love! Take a ride on the little train or a cruise on the 'Yoredale'. A good restaurant for lunch.

BENINGBROUGH HALL (N.T.)
- Hours of Admission: 11:00 to 5:00
- Location; 8 miles northwest of York

   - This imposing Georgian manor was built in 1716. It contains many wonderful details and over 100 pictures on loan from the National Portrait Gallery.
   - The seven acre garden is surrounded by three hundred and seventy acres of informal landscape park.
   - An interesting newly planted walled garden has an archway pergola covered with espalier pears. Half of the area is a kitchen garden with the only organically grown fruits and veggies in the National Trust. You will see a great display of runner beans and a very pretty feature at either end, borders of mixed lavenders.
   - Near the house a wide mixed border contains colorful perennials and roses climbing on the brick walls.
   - Other areas to visit are the American shrub garden, a formal parterre with dahlias and roses, a charming fish pond surrounded by lavenders and a spectacular double herbaceous border.
   - Note: This house is worth a little extra time. Venture inside and enjoy. Ask about the history including a more recent time with the Canadian Air Force. Look for a many wonderful details in moldings and fluted columns and a structural marvel, the cantilevered staircase.

Glorious herbaceous borders and roses climbing on brick walls highlight Beningbrough Hall.

OTHER GARDENS IN THE AREA: STUDLEY ROYAL, RIPLEY CASTLE, HAREWOOD HOUSE

TOUR #17
MAP

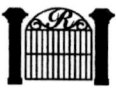

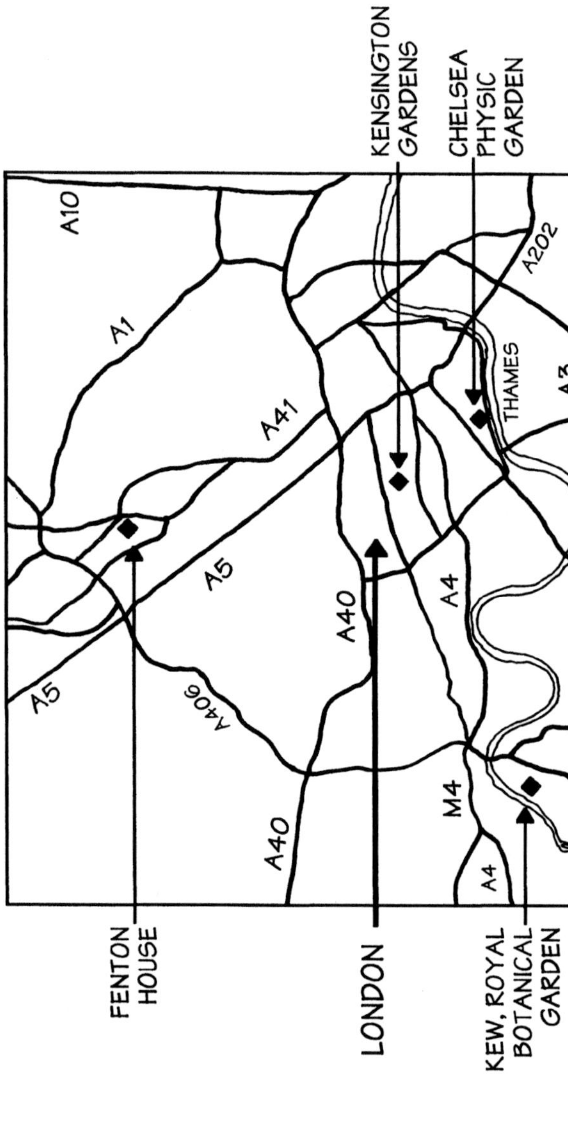

KENSINGTON GARDENS
CHELSEA PHYSIC GARDEN
A10
A1
A41
A202
THAMES
A3
A5
A5
A406
A40
A40
A4
A205
M4
A4
FENTON HOUSE
LONDON
KEW, ROYAL BOTANICAL GARDEN

TOUR #17
* CHELSEA PHYSIC GARDEN
* KENSINGTON GARDENS
* FENTON HOUSE
* KEW, ROYAL BOTANICAL GARDENS

• WEDNESDAY THROUGH SUNDAY •

London has many wonderful places to see not the least of which are the fabulous gardens. You will enjoy the Royal gardens at Kensington Palace where my favorite feature is the sunken garden filled with glorious color from spring through autumn. At Kew, a botanical garden founded by Princess Ausgusta, be sure to visit the fabulous Victorian Palm House and see how many of the 30,000 plants you can identify. You can spend hours at these two gardens. The first rock garden in England was built at Chelsea Physic Garden. One to two hours are needed here. Be sure to watch out for the opening of residential gardens. The charming Fenton House is a good place to start. While you are in London take a few hours to relax and enjoy the gardens.

CHELSEA PHYSIC GARDEN
- Hours of Admission: 2:00 to 5:00
- Location: Swan Walk, Chelsea, London
  - This garden was founded in 1673 by Society of Apothecaries. It is the only garden that retains the title 'Physic' after the old name for the healing arts.
  - After a period of deterioration, in 1712 it was acquired by Sir Hans Sloane, Irish plant collector and physician. Sloane's library and natural history collections became the nucleus of the British Museum when it opened in 1759.
  - Sloane reestablished the garden in 1722 and hired Philip Miller as gardener. During his time at Chelsea, Miller became the greatest botanical horticulturist of the century.
  - In 1733 cotton seed was sent to the colony of Georgia to establish the cotton industry in the New World.
  - In 1771 William Forsyth constructed the first rock garden in England here. He used 40 tons of building stone from the Tower of London as a base to display volcanic rock from Iceland.
  - Today a four acre area contains 4500 different botanical species and one herb garden contains 300 species planted in rectangular beds with brick and grass paths. The plants are set out in order by botanical families.

At Kensington Gardens enjoy the color of the sunken garden from spring to autumn.

KENSINGTON GARDENS
- Hours of Admission: 9:00 to dusk
- Location: Kensington District, London
  - Kensington Palace has stood in the midst of Kensington Gardens since 1690 when Sir Christopher Wren rebuilt the original Nottingham House.
  - It became the home to Kings and Queens starting with William III.
  - Queen Anne, who loved gardening, was responsible for expanding the park and building the Orangery after she took the throne in 1702.
  - George II first opened the gardens to the public. His Queen, Caroline, another avid gardener, installed the Round Pond.
  - One of my favorite features is the glorious sunken. A large rectangular pond is surrounded by stone paving, beds filled with colorful annuals and a perennial border backed by a brick wall. Tulips and daffodils are fabulous in the spring.
  - Note: I have spent many an hour strolling through this wonderful garden in the heart of London. Take a break from those fabulous London restaurants, enjoy a picnic.

FENTON HOUSE (N.T.)
- Hours of Admission: 11:00 to 5:30 Sat & Sun, 2:00 to 5:30 Wed-Fri
- Location: Hampstead Grove, Hampstead underground station
  - Late 17th century Hampstead house is surrounded by a small charming walled and terraced garden.
  - Sunken rose garden provides colorful display in summer.
  - The delightful kitchen garden is filled with a wide selection of veggies.
  - Note: I always enjoy visiting a few London gardens. Keep your ear to the ground for private homes that may be open while you're in town. This garden has gone through a great deal of renovation over the last few years.

KEW, ROYAL BOTANICAL GARDENS
- Hours of Admission: 9:30 to 6:00
- Location: A307 / junction A305 and A205

  - In this three hundred acre garden there are over 30,000 plants that comprise the largest and most diverse collection of living plants in England. Unlike other botanical gardens, it is also truly a lovely landscape.
  - Princess Ausgusta, widow of Frederick, Prince of Wales founded a botanical garden here in 1759.
  - In 1771 Sir Joseph Banks became head of Kew under George III. A series of plant expeditions were conducted during those years which provided a flood of new plants to the garden.
  - Sir William Hooker became the first Director of Kew in 1841 and it was under him that the gardens were open to the public. He was succeeded by his son Joseph in 1865. They were responsible for building the Palm House (1848) and Temperate House (1860-68) which are among the finest glasshouses ever built.
  - The fabulous Victorian Palm House is 2,248 square meters filled with tropical plants from around the world.
  - A formal scented garden is 150 by 40 feet filled with scented herbs and plants. On three sides you will find an arched Laburnum arbor.
  - There are many other wonderful features to enjoy including the Princess of Wales Conservatory, a 17th century style formal parterre, a walled garden with 2000 species of annuals and perennials, a rock garden laid out in 1882 and some specimen trees dating back to the early 18th century.

The fabulous Victorian Palm House at Kew.

Studley Royal Garden

LOTS N' LOTS
OF
HELPFUL
INFORMATION

• GARDEN DESCRIPTIONS •

1. ACORN BANK GARDEN (N.T.)
- 6 miles east of Penrith on A66
Famous for the impressive physic and herb garden, you will find the largest collection of culinary and medical plants in the north. On a warm summer day the fragrance of herbs fills the air. See Tour 12.

2. ASCOTT (N.T.)
- half mile east of Wing on A418
A Rothschild property used by the family as a hunting lodge. The house is surrounded by a garden that combines the early 20th century natural style and Victorian formality.

3. BENINGBROUGH HALL (N.T.)
- 8 miles northwest of York
The imposing Georgian manor is worth visiting after you have enjoyed the many lovely features of the garden. The walled garden contains organically grown fruits and veggies and pretty beds of mixed lavenders while borders near the house display colorful perennials and roses climbing on brick walls. See Tour 16.

4. BRANTWOOD
- south of Coniston
This was the home of social revolutionary, John Ruskin, from 1872 to 1900. Thirty acres of gardens extend from the lake up the hill behind the house and provides beautiful views of the surrounding lake and mountains. See Tour 13.

5. CALKE ABBEY (N.T.)
- 10 miles south of Derby on A514
This Baroque mansion built in 1701 has an extensive walled garden that is under reconstruction. The flower garden and physic garden have been restored to their 18th century beauty.

6. **CANONS ASHBY HOUSE (N.T.)**
   - 2 miles south of Weedon crossroads off A5
   One of the best surviving formal layouts in the style of Henry London and George Wise, this garden provides enjoyment in the small borders, charming topiaries, colorful roses and beautiful views of the countryside. See Tour 6.

7. **CAPEL MANOR**
   - exit 25 of M25, Bullsmoor Lane, Enfield
   This is an ongoing 'garden show'. There are several richly planted demonstration gardens that provide ideas for professionals and amateurs alike.

8. **CASTLE ASHBY**
   - 6 miles east of Northampton, 1.5 miles north of A428
   The 'new' castle was built in 1574 in an 'E' shape to honor Queen Elizabeth I. The formal Italian Garden with clipped hedges, cone shaped topiaries and colorful roses is just one of the lovely features for you to enjoy. See Tour 5.

9. **CHATSWORTH**
   - 2 miles south of Baslow on B6012
   Experience five centuries of British garden history. London and Wise created the grandiose 17th century formal gardens and 'Capability' Brown swept away many of those features in the mid-18th century. Starting in 1826 Joseph Paxton designed many wonderful alterations and additions including the Conservation Wall. Although there are many fabulous features, Chatsworth is famous for The Cascade. Standing at the ornamental pavilion, enjoy the wondrous sights of the fountains, pools and tumbling water of the cascade and glorious views of the countryside. See Tours 8 & 10.

10. **CHELSEA PHYSIC GARDEN**
    - Swan Walk, Chelsea, London
    Founded by Society of Apothecaries in 1673, this four acre garden contains 4500 botanical species including 300 herb species. An interesting collection of plants that provides stimulus for the senses in color and fragrance. See Tour 17.

11. CLAREMONT LANDSCAPE GARDEN (N.T.)
* south edge of Esher, east side of A307
  One of the earliest surviving English landscape gardens, Claremont was touched by the great designers of the time including Vanbrugh, Bridgeman, Kent and Brown. Historically significant. See Tour 1.

12. CLIVEDEN (N.T.)
* 4 miles north of Maidenhead on A4094
  Purchased in 1893 by American, William Waldorf Astor, much of the garden reflects Astor's love for Italian Renaissance gardens. The incredible Fountain of Love adorns the end of the linden lined avenue leading to the house. The view from the terrace is an unbelievable twenty acre parterre and the lovely countryside. This is now a luxury hotel. See Tour 2.

13. CLUMBER PARK
* 4.5 miles southeast of Worksop
  This beautiful parkland surrounding an 80 acre lake is a terrific place for a picnic.

14. COTON MANOR GARDEN
* 9 miles north of Northampton off A428
  Allow plenty of time to enjoy this beautifully designed garden. It is laid out on several levels with many wonderful features including glorious mixed borders, a charming rose garden filled with pink and white roses and peonies, a canopy of trees providing shade for the soothing water garden and a lovely pond. Colorful pots of flowers decorate the paving that connects the garden to the wonderful stone manor house. See Tour 5.

15. COTTESBROOKE HALL
* 10 miles north of Northampton near Creaton on A50
  This magnificent Queen Anne house contains the finest collection of sporting pictures in Europe. Surrounding the hall are lovely herbaceous borders, formal parterres and three hundred year old cedars. The stately Yew Statue Walk provides views over the lake and park.

16. DALEMAIN
- southwest of Penrith on A592

  The manor and the garden have a long, varied history stretching back to the 16th century. One of the finest features is the Tudor Knott Garden, colorful box-edged beds surround a lovely early Roman fountain. See Tour 12.

17. DORNEY COURT
- 25 miles west of London via M4

  An enchanting Tudor manor house, built in 1440, is surrounded by simple gardens of fine clipped hedges, topiaries and colorful mixed borders that compliment the lovely gabled manor.

18. DOVE COTTAGE
- 2.5 miles from Ambleside on A591

  The home of William Wordsworth from 1799-1808 has a charming cottage garden and lovely views over Grasmere onto the fells.

19. ENGLEFIELD HOUSE
- 4 miles west of Reading off A4 and then 3/4 mile on A340 (on left)

  A Deer Park and glorious countryside provide the perfect setting for this terraced garden. Colorful pots on stone railings and mixed borders, created for interesting foliage contrast and the soft colors of roses and perennials are highlights of this garden. You will also find a stream surrounded by boggy plants and a good collection of Japanese maples and English oaks. See Tour 2.

20. FENTON HOUSE (N.T.)
- Hampstead Grove, Hampstead underground station

  A late 17th century manor is surrounded by a charming walled and terraced garden. See Tour 17.

21. GARDENS OF THE ROSE
- 2 miles south of St. Albans

  This is the place for rose lovers everywhere. The Royal National Rose Society garden is filled with thousands of glorious roses. The test beds might even provide information you can take home to your own roses. See Tours 3 & 4.

22. HADDON HALL
- 2.5 miles southeast of Bakewell on A6

Roses are definitely a specialty in this terraced garden. Roses and clematis climb over the stone walls, balustrades and staircases of this medieval manor house. Over 150 varieties create a riot of color and fragrance. You will also find a lovely display of delphiniums in summer. See Tours 8 & 10.

23. HAMPTON COURT
- on the A309 just off A3 at Kingston

This historic palace located on the curve of the Thames, was touched by many of the great designers including Kent, Bridgeman and Brown. It was opened to the public in 1838 by Queen Victoria. Cone shaped yews and mixed borders in the Pond Garden, thirteen spectacular fountains in the Great Fountain Garden and a riot of seasonal color in the sunken garden are three of the many features you will enjoy. See Tour 1.

24. HARDWICK HALL (N.T.)
- 9.5 miles southeast of Chesterfield

You will want to visit the house as well as the garden. This 16th century hunting lodge contains a glorious collection of tapestries and portraits that define several centuries of history. The garden is divided into four sections by allees of yew and hornbeam. There are mixed borders, orchards, shrub roses and a terrific kitchen garden with a big potato patch and standards of hops. See Tours 9 & 10.

25. HAREWOOD HOUSE
- 8 miles north of Leeds at junction of A659 and A61

In 1843 Sir Charles Barry transformed the house from a Georgian country manor to an Italian palazzo. As is befitting such a grand house, the view from the balustrade terrace is a large formal parterre with two lovely fountains and a fabulous sculpture of 'Orphius'. Enjoy a walk along Harewood Lake and you will see a collection of spring flowering shrubs. See Tour 15.

26. HARLOW CARR BOTANICAL GARDENS
- 1.5 miles from Harrogate town center

This 'Wisely of the North' is the headquarters of the Northern Horticultural Society. Spend some time studying plant material and discovering some good ideas for your own garden. See Tours 15 & 16.

27. HATFIELD HOUSE
- 21 miles north of London, A1 juntion 4

John Tradescant, the Elder was the head gardener and designer of the original 17th century formal garden. Swept away for the parkland style in the mid-18th century, the formal garden was recreated over the last twenty-five years from Tradescant's notes. There are many lovely features including a wonderful sunken knot garden which is viewed from a terrace above. See Tour 3.

28. HOLDENBY HOUSE
- 6 miles northwest of Northampton off A428

Only remnants of the 16th century formal garden and grand palace survive today. What you will find is a charming herb garden designed by Rosemary Verey, colorful roses mixed with fruits and veggies in the kitchen garden and an interesting 19th century manor. See Tour 5.

29. HOLEHIRD
- on A592, 1 mile north of junction with A591

A fabulous botanical garden in the heart of the Lake District. You will find a wonderful collection of planting beds and glorious views of the countryside. See Tour 13.

30. HOLKER HALL
- 4 miles southwest of Grange-over-Sands on B5277

What you see today is a house in the grandest Victorian style and a woodland garden mixed with 19th century formal features designed by Joseph Paxton. Borders in soft pinks and blues of perennials, old fashion roses and peonies, clipped hedges and big pots overflowing with color create a formal effect. The woodlands abound with thousands of bulbs and spring flowering shrubs. See Tour 11.

31. HUGHENDEN MANOR (N.T.)
- 1.5 miles north of High Wycombe on A4128

A five acre Victorian garden surrounds the Gothic home of Prime Minister Benjamin Disraeli from 1847 to his death in 1881. Favorites of Mrs. Disraeli, pelargoniums and blue agapanthus are still found everywhere especially in the fabulous parterre.

32. HUTTON-IN-THE-FOREST
- 7 miles northwest of Penrith on B5305

As the name implies, Hutton is surrounded by the woodland of the medieval Forest of Inglewood. A large walled garden is designed in a series of rooms with soft colored herbaceous borders, 'Fairy' roses and a charming dovecoat. See Tour 12.

33. KEDLESTON HALL (N.T.)
- 5 miles northwest of Derby on A52

A garden in the natural style of the mid-18th century surrounds this fabulous neo-classical house based on the villas of architect Palladio. The Long Walk provides extensive views of the countryside to the south while the pleasure grounds, formalized by Edwin Lutyens and Gertrude Jekyll, provide simple, colorful planting. See Tour 7.

34. KENSINGTON GARDENS
- Kensington District, London

A lovely place in the middle of the hub-bub of London to enjoy a stroll or maybe a picnic. Big trees, flowering shrubs and fabulous sunken gardens filled with colorful annuals from spring to fall. See Tour 17.

35. KEW, ROYAL BOTANICAL GARDENS
- A307/junction A305 and A205

A botanical garden was first founded here in 1759 by Princess Augusta. The garden was the recipient of many plants from Plant Expeditions in the mid-18th century. The wonderful Palm House was built in 1848 and is filled with tropical plants from around the world. See Tour 17.

36. KNEBWORTH HOUSE
- 30 miles north of central London, from A1 at junction 7

  Charles Dickens and Winston Churchill were frequent visitors to this Gothic style house. The formal Victorian gardens were designed and simplified by Edwin Lutyens in 1911. Enjoy the herb garden designed by Gertrude Jekyll, the Yellow Garden and a canopy of 'Fairy' roses. See Tour 3.

37. LEIGHTON HALL
- 10 miles from exit 35 on M6

  Situated in a parkland with the panorama of the Lakeland Falls behind it, the grey limestone walls of this manor stand out beautifully against the green of the land. The garden has a long colorful herbaceous border, rose covered brick walls, a caterpillar maze and a spring flowering woodland walk.

38. LEVENS HALL
- 5 miles south of Kendal on A6

  An amazing assortment of shapes, sizes and forms clipped from boxwoods and yews create Topiary Town. This world famous topiary garden was first laid out in 1694 and has largely remained unaltered because the family refused to give in to the 'naturalistic' style of the 18th century. Topiaries are everywhere including in the parterres where 15,000 plants are used as bedding plants and are changed twice a year. See Tour 11.

39. LOTHERTON HALL
- 3.5 miles northeast of Garforth on B1217

  Created in the early part of this century, this garden is the home to tender plants, rare to this northern area. An outstanding sculpture of a Chinese priest stands in a bed of peonies on one terrace. A rectangular rose garden enclosed by yew hedges provides quite a fragrance to the garden in high summer. See Tour 15.

40. MELBOURNE HALL
- 8 miles south of Derby on A514

May be the only existing formal garden of the early 18th century by Henry Wise left in England; others were lost to the landscape phase. A grand expanse of lawn leads to the Great Basin which spreads out before the exquisite wrought iron 'Birdcage' created in 1706. See Tour 7.

41. MUNCASTER CASTLE
- 1 mile east of Ravenglass on a595

Thirty meters above sea level, this pink granite castle has wonderful views of the Lakeland Fells and a rhododendron filled valley. Stroll through this seventy-seven acre woodland garden and enjoy many delightful walks lined with colorful azaleas, camellias and rhododendrons.

42. MYDDELTON HOUSE GARDENS
- junction of M25 and A10, on Bulls Cross, Enfield

This was the creation and home of famous plantsman, E.A. Bowles. You will find a collection of rare and unique plants. Visit in the spring and enjoy a riot of color from millions of bulbs. See Tour 3.

43. NEWBY HALL
- 4 miles west of A1 toward Ripon

What a sight, six hundred of feet of colorful double borders stretch from the Queen Anne house to the River Ure. These glorious gardens began to take form in 1920 and were influenced by Lawrence Johnston and Hidcote. You will enjoy Sylvia's Garden, soothing water sounds and shrub roses in the Rose Garden, the Autumn Garden filled with late flowering perennials and the Victorian Rock Garden. See Tours 14 & 16.

44. NEWSTEAD ABBEY
- 12 miles north of Nottingham along A60

This was the historic home of poet, Lord Byron. The old walled kitchen garden is now filled with glorious old-fashioned roses. If you venture out from the walled garden you will find an early 20th century Japanese garden, a large colorful iris garden and a sunken pool surrounded by terraced lawn. See Tours 7 & 9.

45. PARCEVALL HALL GARDEN
- 9 miles north of Skipton; 7 miles off A59 at Bolton Abbey

A surprise in the middle of nowhere. This 16th century stone house is surrounded by a wonderful terraced garden and incredible countryside. The top terrace contains mixed borders planted in pastel shades with a lovely round pond while the third terrace provides an alcove, a place to enjoy views out to the hills and valleys. See Tour 14.

46. RENISHAW HALL
- 6 miles equidistant from Sheffield & Chesterfield on A616

Situated in the foothills of the Pennines we found a wonderful 19th century Italianesque garden. The garden is designed in a series of descending terraces filled with clipped hedges, rambling roses, topiaries and, as you might expect, Italian statues. The shapes, forms and countryside views provide many opportunities for photos. See Tours 8 & 9.

47. RYDAL MOUNT
- 1.5 miles from Ambleside on A591

The home of William Wordsworth from 1813 until his death in 1850. Four and a half acres of glorious gardens created by the poet provide a spectacular display of color in spring and beautiful views to the countryside. See Tour 13.

48. SAVILL GARDEN
- Wick Lane, englefield Green, signposted from Ascot & Windsor

Set in Windsor Great Park, this 20th century woodland garden is designed to provide color and beauty throughout the year. An unusual feature, several impressive borders are large in scale to accommodate much larger plants. Queen Elizabeth Temperate House, constructed in 1994 to house tender plants, is very well done in both architecture and planting. Valley Garden, four hundred acres of lovely woodlands, is walking distance from Savill. See Tour 2.

49. SIZERGH CASTLE (N.T.)
- 3.5 miles south of Kendal

  An impressive 14th century Pele Tower forms the core of this castle which has been the home for the Strickland family for over 750 years. Enjoy the imposing limestone rock garden planted in 1926, a one hundred yard fuchsia walk and vibrant color from spring bulbs and fall foliage. See Tour 11.

50. STOWE LANDSCAPE GARDEN (N.T.)
- 3 miles northwest of Buckingham off A422

  May be the most important landscape gardens in Britain. Initially formal in design, the garden was started in the 16th century by Sir Richard Temple who spent 40 years and a great deal of money creating his dream. In the 18th century the Temple family employed many leading architects, landscape architects and sculptors including Vanbrugh, Bridgeman, Kent and Brown who created a landscape in the new naturalistic style of the period. The National Trust acquired the property in 1989 and has embarked on one of the most ambitious and expensive programs of garden restoration ever undertaken in Britain. See Tour 6.

51. STUDLEY ROYAL and FOUNTAINS ABBEY (N.T.)
- 4 miles west of Ripon off B6265

  An incredible one hundred and fifty acre water garden that flows from the ominous ruins of the 12th century Fountains Abbey along the canal over cascades into the lake in the park. See Tour 14.

52. SULGRAVE MANOR
- 7 miles from junction 11 of M40 off B4525

  A little American history, this was the early home of George Washington's ancestors. The attractive gardens were designed in 1921. See Tour 6.

53. SWISS GARDEN
- 1.5 miles west of Biggleswade A1 roundabout

  The design of this early 19th century was inspired by all things Swiss. This is largely a spring garden filled with masses of daffodils and lush rhododendrons and azaleas. See Tour 4.

54. WISLEY GARDEN
- off A3 near Woking

This is the world famous 240 acre garden of the Royal Horticultural Society. There are several wonderful features including a large terraced pond filled with water lilies, an extensive rock garden built up the side of the hill, a herb garden surrounded by a hornbeam hedge and a huge rose garden that is divided into four glorious sections. See Tour 1.

55. WREST PARK & GARDENS
- 1 mile east of Silsoe off A6

As you enter the garden from this 19th century mansion you will be transformed back in time. The dominant feature is the Great Garden, a magnificent canal laid out in the early 18th century which leads you to a fabulous Pavilion. Soothing water sounds from the cascade fill the air near the rustic bath house. See Tour 4.

• BIOGRAPHIES OF GARDENERS •

John Aislabie (1670-1742)
Most notable work: Studley Royal, Yorkshire
- In 1716 Aislabie rebuilt the house at Studley Royal in the classical style. There is no evidence of an architect and it is presumed the work was his.
- He was appointed Chancellor of the Exchequer in 1718 which crowned an ambitious political career. He was involved in a scandal surrounding the South Sea Company and his term as Chancellor and his political career ended in 1721. He retired to his estate at Studley Royal.
- His landscape design, unique for its time, was greatly influenced by his friend, Sir John Vanbrugh.
- The setting for landscape was the River Skell valley between steeply wooded sides of Fountains Abbey past the park surrounding Studley for a distance of one mile. It is independent of the house and depends on its own qualities for success.
- He was not able to acquire Fountains Abbey during his lifetime.
- His son, William succeeded in buying the Abbey in 1768. He was able to bring his father's work to its desired conclusion by landscaping the abbey vista.
- William turned down 'Capability' Brown's suggestion that he should complete the design and, instead, carried out the work himself.

Sir Joseph Banks (1743-1820)
Most notable works: Kew, Royal Botanical Gardens, London
- Born of a wealthy family, Banks declared his passion for botany at a very early age. He is considered among the most important botanists of the 18th century.
- In 1766 he traveled to Labrador and Newfoundland to collect plants
- Banks accompanied Captain Cook on his first voyage to the South Seas, 1768-71. Hundreds of, as yet unknown, plants were brought back from this trip.
- He became the head of Kew in 1771 under George III. He was President of the Royal Society for 42 years beginning in 1778. He was knighted in 1781.

Sir Charles Barry (1795-1860)
Most notable works: Harewood House, Yorkshire; Cliveden, Buckinghamshire; Trentham Park, Staffordshire
- The most influential figure for Italianate terraced gardens in mid-Victorian England. Many of his garden designs survive but have been greatly simplified.
- In 1833 the 2nd Duke of Sutherland commissioned him to rebuild Trentham Park in Staffordshire. The present house at Cliveden, also owned by the Duke, was designed by Barry in 1851.
- In 1843 Barry was commissioned to provide the foreground for a 'Capability' Brown landscape at Harewood House.
- At Harewood he designed the terrace garden, an intricate parterre that was built around three fountain pools and provided a commanding view of Brown's parkland.
- He was knighted in 1852 in recognition for his work on the new Houses of Parliament.

Guillaume Beaumont (1650-1729)
Most notable work: Levens Hall, Cumbria
- Little is known about this fine designer who was born in France.
- He was commissioned to work on Levens Hall by the owner, his friend James Grahme. Beaumont moved to a modest house there in 1692 and lived most of the rest of his life at Levens.
- Although he advised on several English gardens, including Hampton Court, all evidence of this work is gone. The world famous topiary garden at Levens Hall is the only existing example of his work.
- He also created a 'bastion' or a short ditch and retaining wall which was to become known as a 'ha-ha', a radical innovation providing an unbroken visual link between garden and the countryside. See the glossary for a definition of 'ha-ha'.

E.A. Bowles (1865-1954)
Most notable works: Myddelton House Gardens, Middlesex
- Bowles was a gardener, writer and enthusiastic plant collector.
- He had a passion for unusual varieties and you will find many of these in his home garden at Myddelton.

- In 1889 he made his first plant expedition to Italy.
- He wrote a trilogy of garden books 'My Garde in Spring', My Garden In Summer' and "My Garden in Autumn and Winter".

Charles Bridgeman (d. 1738)
Most notable works: Claremont, Surrey; Chiswick House, London; Kensington Gardens, London; Rousham House, Oxfordshire; Stowe, Buckinghamshire
- He helped bridge the gap between the formality of the late 17th century and the emerging 'landscape' period.
- His style retained the details and characteristics of formality but was asymmetrical and presented a relationship between the garden and the surrounding countryside.
- A practical gardening knowledge and his professional training as a surveyor which enabled him to cope with large scale designs were his two main assets. He could convert ideas onto paper and then into reality.
- He was a pupil of George London & Henry Wise, the leading gardening partnership during the reign of William & Mary.
- Much of his work was altered or destroyed by 'Capability' Brown and others during the 'Landscape Movement'.
- He worked on Stowe & Claremont with Sir John Vanbrugh and was greatly influenced by his style. Bridgeman continued to work at Stowe from 1715 until shortly before his death in 1738.
- Although Rousham Park is acknowledged as William Kent's most outstanding work, he did work closely within the framework of Bridgeman's original layout. Some of Bridgeman's features still remain such as the 'natural theater' and the bowling green lawn.
- He is considered by many to be the first to use the 'ha-ha' in England.
- In 1728 he succeeded Wise as the royal gardener and retained that position until his death.

Lancelot "Capability" Brown (1716-1783)
Most notable works: too numerous to list them all but those included in this book are: Stowe, Buckinghamshire; Castle Ashby, Northamptonshire; Chatsworth, Derbyshire; Harewood House, Yorkshire; Wrest Park, Bedfordshire

Brown (continued)
- Even after 200 years, Brown's stamp on the English countryside remains unmistakable. His work was so close to nature that, since the landscapes have now reached maturity, it is indistinguishable.
- He did destroy many lovely gardens but he did create many fine landscapes and established a garden style that belonged to Britain alone.
- During his 40 year career he refined the concept of landscape so that it became dependent on three simple factors: trees, water, terrain.
- His ideal landscape had gentle contours, water and a minimum of man-made interruptions. To achieve his goal he planted thousands of native trees, moved huge qualities of earth and damned streams to create lakes.
- Brown took the job as head gardener at Stowe when he was in his twenties. He learned from the work of William Kent and eventually contributed to the last two major phases of Stowe's development.
- By the time Brown left Stowe (after 9 years), he had already completed several commissions and had established himself as the leading landscape designer of the day.
- In his redesign of Warwick Castle, he removed the small formal gardens and replaced them with lawn.
- He was appointed surveyor to His Majesty's gardens and waters at Hampton Court in 1764.

William Sawrey Gilpin (1762-1843)
Most notable works: Clumber Park, Nottinghamshire; Scotney Castle, Kent
- Gilpin was the last major advocate of the 'picturesque movement' before it became absorbed by the Victorian era.
- At Scotney Castle he created one of the most acclaimed landscapes of the 'pictuesque movement'. On his advice the new house was built on top of the hill looking down on the castle ruins.
- In 1832 he published *Practical Hints for Landscape Gardeners*.

Gertrude Jekyll (1843-1932)
Most notable works: too numerous to list but a few examples are Knebworth House, Hertfordshire; Kedleston Hall, Derbyshire; Marsh Court, Hampshire; Munstead Wood, Surry; Woodside, Buckinghamshire
- Jekyll made an unequaled contribution to the foundation of gardens as we know them today. She demonstrated how gardening could best be scaled down in a modest home without sacrificing on quality or interest.
- She helped to bridge the gap between professional and amateur gardeners and promoted the involvement of women.
- A simple portrait of Jekyll indicates she was trained as a painter and worked as a craftswoman. She had an encyclopedic memory of both wild and cultivated plants and a fondness for the simple life.
- Preferring the small and intimate to the large and expansive, she paid attention to detail in plant color, in form and in architectural materials.
- A friendship and working relationship developed between Jekyll and Edwin Lutyens. The most fruitful years of their partnership were 1897 to 1908.
- Certain guidelines and techniques were constants in all Jekyll and Lutyen's work together: 1) unity between house and garden, 2) between planting and architectural features, 3) between various areas of the garden.
- Unfortunately, little of her work remains in its original form.
- She began her writing career in the 1870's with magazine articles in *The Garden* and she wrote her first book in 1899.

Major Lawrence Johnston (1871-1958)
Most notable work: Hidcote Manor, Gloucestershire
- Johnston was an American, who was born in Paris, educated in England and became a naturalized British citizen in 1900.
- The farm at Hidcote was purchased for him by his mother on his return from the war in South Africa.
- He had no practical experience or professional training but he did have a clear idea of how the garden should evolve.
- Johnston was able to indulge his acquired skills and knowledge of plants in all the different planting beds he created. He enclosed those beds with a variety of hedges including hollies, yews, beeches and hornbeams.

Johnston (continued)
- He joined two plant collecting expeditions between 1907 and 1914, the first to southern Africa, the second to Yunnan in China.

William Kent (1685-1748)
Most notable works: Claremont, Surrey; Chiswick House, London; Rousham House, Oxfordshire; Stowe, Buckinghamshire
- He initiated the change known as the 'landscape' movemen at the beginning of the 18th century.
- Horace Walpole called him "The father of modern gardening. He leapt the fence and saw that all nature was a garden." The influence of Kent's garden designs was enormous through the balance of the 18th century and beyond.
- Although we consider him a painter, landscape gardener and architect, he was more architect as seen from the structures (temples, obelisks, gateways) he put into his plans.
- He had a more visual approach to design. There is no evidence that he drew up plans or wrote down his ideas (except in letters) which allowed him to create with a greater freshness.
- Kent spent nine years in Italy starting in his late twenties. The architecture, paintings and gardens he studied there were a great inspiration to him throughout his career.
- Probably the most significant influence to his career as a landscape architect was Alexander Pope who believed that "all gardening is landscape painting".
- He added his own ideas to the designs of Bridgeman at Stowe, Rousham and Claremont. Rousham is considered Kent's masterpiece.

George London (d. 1713)
Most notable works: Hampton Court, London; Blenheim Palace, Oxfordshire; Melbourne Hall, Derbyshire
- In 1681 London established Brompton Nurseries, the first English commercial nursery. He was joined by Henry Wise in 1687.
- The partnership of London & Wise was the foremost designer of formal gardens during the reigns of William & Mary and Queen Anne.
- Influences from Italy and France were incorporated into the English landscape.

- The formality of the hedges and the intricate patterns of gardens beds they created at places like Blenheim Palace caused some of the strongest reactions from members of the landscape movement.
- Unfortunately much of their work disappeared in the face of that more naturalistic style of the 18th century.

Sir Edwin Lutyens (1869-1944)
Most notable works: too numerous to provide a total list but a few examples are: Abbotswood, Gloucestershire; Heathcote, Yorkshire; Putteridge Park, Bedfordshire
- One of the most original and sought-after architects of his time.
- He met Gertrude Jekyll when he was just 20 and his education as an architect was influenced in such a manner to set him apart from his contemporaries.
- His partnership with Jekyll created a wonderful harmony between house and garden, a place to live in, a place to enjoy. The balance they sought formed a cornerstone for 20th century gardens.
- In later years Lutyens developed a more individual and classical style demonstrated in the grand formal canal gardens he created after World War I.
- His garden architecture stressed the importance of strong directional lines and horizontal and vertical surfaces again demonstrated in his strong hedges.
- He created some of the best known garden furniture designs of the early 20th century.

William Morris (1834-1896)
- Morris was a designer and decorator, a creator of wonderful textiles, a poet and political activist and the 'creator' of the Arts & Crafts Movement of the 19th Century.
- He rebelled against the Victorian period and his own privileged upbringing and grew to believe in the simplicities of life.
- His concept of the ideal home was: "Have nothing in your houses that you do not know to be useful, or believe to be beautiful."
- In 1861 he set up the Morris & Co. firm, a decorating company that provided not only decorating services but products such as fabrics and wallpapers.

Sir Joseph Paxton (1803-1865)
Most notable works: Chatsworth, Derbyshire; Somerleyton, Suffolk; Birkenhead Park, Merseyside
- Paxton brought to the world of horticulture all the integral characteristics of the mid-Victorian style in England.
- He was a gardener, architect, engineer, town planner, railway director & Member of Parliament but his most lasting contribution was as a gardener.
- He began as a gardener at Chatsworth in 1826 and remained until 1858. He made a tremendous contribution to the architectural features and the planting you see today; the estate became as much his domain as the owner.
- On a hill east of the house Paxton built an aqueduct which provided water for a fabulous waterfall, water and power for several fountains and even some power for the house.
- He perfected the construction of glass houses. The two at Chatsworth became wonders of the Victorian age. One, the Conservatory, built between 1836 and 1840, was the largest glasshouse in the world.
- In 1843, he designed the first town park with public access at Birkenhead Park, Liverpool. It provided inspiration for public gardens in England, Europe and America.
- He was awarded knighthood in 1851 and became a member of Parliament from 1854 until his death.

Beatrix Potter (1866-1943)
Most notable works: Peter Rabbit; Hill Top, Cumbria
- Ms. Potter is the renowned creator of Peter Rabbit and his enchanting friends.
- She also developed a great love for the northern countryside. Her passion to protect the Lake District prompted her to play an active role in founding the National Trust.
- Although London born, she made frequent visits to the Lake District beginning at age of 16 in 1882. The beauty of the area made a lasting impression on the young girl and 23 years latter, in 1905, she bought Hill Top in Cumbria.
- Hill Top became her first garden. A romantic cottage garden, it inspired several books and can be found in her paintings.

- She also purchased Cockshott Point on the shores of Lake Windermere in 1927 and the Monk Coniston in 1930. When she died in 1943, her estate included 14 farms, 8 cottages and 4000 acres of land. The entire estate was left in the care of the National Trust.

Humphry Repton (1752-1818)
Most notable works: too numerous to list but a few examples are: Harewood House, Yorkshire; Mulgrave Castle, Yorkshire
- 'Capability' Brown's successor, he adapted the "landscape movement" to the emerging prosperous middle class. He added "practicality" to Kent and Brown's ideas.
- In 1788, in his late 30's, with little formal training, he turned from architecture to garden design out of financial necessity. In a very short time he had a busy and successful career with recommendations from many satisfied clients.
- For Repton four requisites were needed for a perfect landscape design: 1) design must hide natural defects and display natural beauties, 2) boundaries should be carefully hidden or disguised, 3) the look should be natural, 4) objects of convenience or comfort must be removed or concealed if it isn't possible to make them part of the general scenery.
- He sited houses near the buildings (barns, stables, etc.) that serviced the household and he felt that the style of the house should be closely reflected in the style of its surroundings.
- He had a feeling for the use of plants and a knowledge of their appropriateness to compliment various architectural styles.
- He reintroduced the terrace and, to a certain extent, flowers to the garden.
- A 'Red Book' system for presenting proposals to each client was created.
- Like so many others, much of his work has either disappeared or been seriously altered.

John Ruskin 1819-1900
- Born in London and educated at Oxford, this British writer was also an art critic, and reformer.
- The major theme of his writings was the relationship between art and morality.
- Ruskin was a critic of the aesthetic and social effects of the industrial revolution and his later writings influenced social reform in Great Britain for several generations.

Graham Stuart Thomas (1909-)
Most notable works: Champion of Old Fashioned Roses
- Thomas has been the champion of old fashioned shrub roses and has been largely responsible for their return to popularity.
- He is a plantsman, designer, painter, historian and journalist who studied horticulture at Cambridge University Botanic Garden.
- As garden adviser for the National Trust from 1955 to 1974, he masterminded a number of outstanding garden restorations such as: Claremont Landscape Garden and Westbury Court.
- In 1972 he designed a rose garden for the National Trust at Mottisfont Abbey. The collection of old fashioned roses that he began to build after the war provided the nucleus for this internationally famous garden.
- He has written a series of books on roses, including *The Old Shrub Roses (1995)* which remains his most popular. He has also written books on perennials and ground covers among others.

John Tradescant the Elder 1570-1638
Most notable works: Hatfield House, Hertfordshire; Cranborne Manor, Dorset
- One of the founding figures of British gardening, he rose from obscure origins to become the most important and influential gardener of his time. He was Keeper of His Majesty's Gardens under Charles I.
- First in a distinguished line of men who were both knowledgeable horticulturists and garden designers, the Elder became the first official plant collector. In 1618 he became the first English botanist to travel to Russia.
- Some of the most significant plants collected were from North America. Although he never traveled there himself, he did send his son in 1637.
- He was a part of the Virginia Company, which was responsible for the financing and transportation of new trees and plants to England.
- Hatfield House is one of his only two surviving works. The general design and all of the planting were under his control. Although many changes have taken place over the years, the present Lady Salisbury has taken great pains to restore it to its original beauty.

Sir John Vanbrugh (1664-1726)
Most notable works: Claremont, Surrey; Queen's Theatre, London; Stowe, Buckinghamshire
- Vanbrugh was a soldier, a playwrite and, finally, an architect.
- He developed a style of baroque architecture that was unique in England.
- The idea that gardens, like painted landscapes, are composed of lakes, temples, woods and vistas was first conceived by Vanbrugh.
- He was committed to a strongly structured, balanced, geometric plan.
- He worked with Charles Bridgeman on Claremont and Stowe. Unfortunately, out of all the garden buildings he designed at Stowe only the rotunda still survives.

Rosemary Verey (1918-)
Most notable works: Barnsley House, Gloucestershire; Holdenby House, Northamptonshire
- One of the best known contemporary garden authorities in England. Mrs. Verey exemplifies the manor in which 'amateur' gardeners and garden writers have influenced today's garden.
- The foundations of her garden work are a fascination with garden history and a love of plants.
- She has had great success incorporating period features from Tudor and 17th century gardens into a modern design.
- Since 1980 she has written several books on garden design and style.
- Barnsley House, her best known work and her home, has provided much of the research and material for her books.

Ellen Willmott 1858-1934
Most notable works: Warley Place, Essex
- Her Friend, Gertrude Jekyll, described her as 'the greatest of living women gardeners'.
- She was also fanatical about music- she sang well and was an accomplished violinist- and a talented painter, photographer, wood turner and printer.
- Of her generation no one was more knowledgeable about plants and how to grow them.
- At its peak, her home garden at Warley Place contained an unbelievable collection of 100,000 species and varieties of plants and employed 104 gardeners.

Willmott (continued)
- in 1890 she acquired a chateau in Provence. This was home to her collection of 11,000 roses.
- She was a generous donor of plants to Kew and to Wisley.
- She provided financial support for many plant expeditions to China and eastern Russia.
- Her reckless spending over many years finally caught up with her, she had to sell her estates in France and Italy and after 1918, Warley was run with a skeleton staff. It never returned to its pre-war brilliance. Warley Place with its magnificent gardens does not exist today.

• GARDEN DESIGN PERIODS •

FORMAL GARDEN DESIGN

In the 16th Century the pleasure garden began to appear. Instead of being a place to just look at, it became a place to spend time in, to entertain in and to enjoy. The garden layout or design was rigid, symetrical and formal with knots, hedges and colorful flowers. There were tennis courts, bowling greens and imitation animals.

In the 17th Century, design was influenced by the Renaissance. Many of the garden designers of this period were French, i.e.: the Huguenot Brothers and Isaac de Caus. The concept was that the house and garden should compliment each other. Most of the grand gardens of the pre-Civil War period were enclosed by walls and there was little connection with the surrounding landscape.

An increasing interest in the horticultural side of gardening developed during this time. This was demonstrated by the creation of the Oxford Botanical Garden in 1621 and the success of plant collectors such as John Tradescant and his son John who traveled not only to the continent but to the New World.

The Jacobeans and the Stuarts brought gardening to a fine art. One's garden became a reflection of one's status. Fountains and water features were used and topiaries became popular once again.

During the Restoration, in the later half of the 17th Century, the aristocracy brought back ideas from their travels in Europe and the French style was at its height. Smaller landowners began to take an interest in gardening. There was an increasing importance placed in the relationship between garden and surrounding countryside even during this period. This was to lay some of the foundation for the "landscape movement".

It was obvious that the New World had a wealth of horticultural treasures. The most extensive collection of North American trees and shrubs in England was acquired by Henry Compton

Formal Design (continued)

for his garden at Fulham Palace. Compton, an influential figure in the plant trade, employed George London as gardener for several years starting in 1681.

The Dutch influence was also very popular. Their designs were geometric in their formality but smaller in scale than the French. The Dutch had also established themselves as plantsmen without equal and they displayed a true enjoyment in flower gardening.

Even with all these influences from Europe and America, England retained a clear measure of independence. Although much of what was created during this period was dramatically changed or even destroyed during the "Landscape Movement", the groundwork for England's future influence in the gardening field was established.

A few of the gardeners of the period were Charles Bridgeman, William Kent, George London and Henry Wise and Sir John Vanbrugh.

"LANDSCAPE MOVEMENT"- THE NATURAL LOOK

The Landscape Movement began in the early 18th Century and coincided with the Georgian period of architecture. It was a reaction to the formality and contrivances of the 17th century (topiaries, knot gardens, parterres) and a social reaction to the monarchy in favor of the landed gentry.

A respect for nature, "an essential factor of human life", became part of the philosophy of the time. It was felt that gardens should take their inspiration from nature. The garden became part of the countryside and the countryside came into the garden. Geometrical symmetry was replaced by asymmetry and serpentine curves.

Craftsmanship was also a part of the movement; wrought iron work was transformed into decorative gates and arbors and there were finely worked lead statues and urns.

The second half of the 18th Century was clearly dominated by Lancelot "Capability" Brown who carried the movement to an extreme. He created hundreds of acres of landscape parks. Hundreds of tons of dirt were moved to create a "natural" look, rivers were diverted or dammed and hills were built or removed. Hedges, parterres and flowers were removed, walls and fences were replaced by ha-has and architectural monuments became an integral part of the landscape.

Although horticulture took a backseat during this period, there was a continuing exchange of plant materials and ideas between England and the United States. The first varieties of rhododendrons and several ornamental trees and shrubs were imported from North America.

In the later part of the 18th Century, the "picturesque" movement developed. The preference was for a landscape of the natural scenery of mountains, streams and woodlands. This was again a reaction, but this time to Brown and his artificial landscapes.

Near the turn of the century Humphry Repton, who had initially followed in Brown's footsteps, was responsible for a transitional period when ornamental flower gardens and terraces were reintroduced into the "landscape".

A few of the gardeners of the period from England and the United States were Lancelot "Capability" Brown, Thomas Jefferson, Humphry Repton, George Washington.

VICTORIAN PERIOD

This was the real beginning of the English passion for gardening. The formal garden of the 17th century was reinstated. Huge and elaborate gardens were designed to compliment the flamboyant mansions of the period. Small cottage gardens became popular with the more prosperous middle class and even the working class had their window boxes.

The industrial revolution played a part in the new garden design. Coal furnaces heated greenhouses and the brick walls

Victorian Period (continued)

of kitchen gardens. Steam engines provided the power for garden fountains. The removal of the glass tax in 1845 opened the door to the building of conservatories and greenhouses. In addition, the wealth accumulated from industrial and commercial enterprises provided the money to create the great houses and gardens of this period.

The plant trade continued to grow. David Douglas introduced conifers from the United States, rhododendrons were introduced from the Himalayas and the fashionable scented-leafed geraniums were imported from South Africa.

This was the start of new gardening magazines and books, new kinds of garden tools and the first lawn mower which was invented in 1830.

Lawn was an essential element (made easier by the mower), roses were an important part of all the big estates and rock gardens were all the rage.

Americans greatly admired the public parks and gardens of the Victorian Period. F.L. Olmsted, an American landscape architect, visited England in 1850. His designs for parks such as Central Park in New York were greatly influenced by what he saw during his visit.

The Victorian influence remains in England today through the public parks and the colorful window boxes, hanging baskets and pots of geraniums, lobelia and aubretia seen throughout the country.

A few of the gardeners of the period were Humphry Repton, Sir Joseph Paxton, Sir Charles Barry, Frederick Law Olmsted.

ARTS & CRAFTS MOVEMENT

In the last part of the 19th century in England, the Arts & Crafts Movement developed as a reaction to the ostentations of the Victorian period. It was a desire to emphasize craftsmanship, the qualities of the rural life and a more natural style.

At the center of the movement was designer William Morris who formed William Morris & Co. in 1861 with the goal of revitalizing the arts through craftsmanship. Morris, who was very fond of the Cotswolds, encouraged his friends to move there and a large number of craftsmen did move to Chipping Camden at the turn of the century

Munstead Wood in Surrey, designed by Edwin Lutyens for Gertrude Jekyll, is a good example of the movement. It incorporated Bargate stone walls, handmade tiles and mullion windows. Another example is Great Dixter in Kent which was designed by Christopher Lloyd.

EARLY 20th CENTURY

The garden once again became social, a place for activity. It was no longer a place to merely be looked upon from the house but was something to be lived in, a continuation of the house with outdoor rooms.

The reaction to the Victorian garden took many forms. One was informal, a return to the natural look (the A & C Movement); another was formal in the overall look of the architecture and the garden. The third form provided a balance between architecture and horticulture, had an attention to details and could be adapted to any scale.

The biggest advocate for informality and more natural planting was William Robinson. Although a gardener in his own right, he was primarily a writer who had much influence on the designs of the day and on the future work of people like Gertrude Jekyll.

The model for the more formal gardens was the Italian Renaissance. Harold Peto and the water garden he designed at Buscot Park and Achille Duchene's water terrace at Blenheim Palace are good examples of this style.

The most lasting garden style was established by Gertrude Jekyll & Edwin Lutyens. Their gardens did not require expansive acreage and settings to achieve the desired affect and they demonstrated that the garden could have several looks

Early 20th Century (continued)

throughout the year. They focused on regional architecture, local materials and placed a strong emphasis on plantsmanship. Future generations of designers and gardeners in England and America have followed their example and guidelines.

A few of the gardeners of the period were Gertrude Jekyll, Edwin Lutyens, Lawrence Johnston, Harold Peto, William Robinson, Achille Duchene.

MID 20th CENTURY

In the post World War I period, people did more of the gardening themselves. They looked for designs that were more understated and displayed planting rather than architectural monuments.

In the United States, Frank Lloyd Wright developed the "Prairie School" of architecture. During that same time Jans Jensen's garden designs became known as the "prairie style". An important part of his designs was his use of trees and plants that were native to a particular area.

In England a desire for informality was expressed in the creation of natural woodland gardens. Native trees, flowering and ornamental trees and shrubs and spring bulbs extended a garden's life throughout most of the year. The garden at the Rothschild estate, Exbury, was created during this period. Begun in 1919, it is over 200 acres of woodlands with a remarkable collection of rhododendrons and azaleas.

For most people, however, the typical 20th Century garden did not require hundreds of acres or famous designers. The style was 'compartments', outdoor rooms with walls or hedges created out of hollies, yews or hornbeams as Lawrence Johnston did at Hidcote and 'Vita' Sackville-West did at Sissinghurst. The look was colorful borders with roses and perennials.

A few of the gardeners of the period were Lawrence Johnston, 'Vita' Sackville-West, Thomas Church, Jans Jensen.

LATE 20th CENTURY

These are the days of the gifted "amateur" gardeners such as Penelope Hobhouse (one of my favorites), Christopher Lloyd and Rosemary Verey who, through their own gardens and their books and lectures, have reached a wider audience than many "professionals".

Garden styles have been borrowed from the past and mixed together with great freedom to create individual design and charm.

A few of the gardeners of the period are Penelope Hobhouse, Geoffrey Jellicoe, Christopher Lloyd, Rosemary Verey.

• GLOSSARY OF TERMS •

Allee- a formal hedged walk or road within the "wilderness". Yew and hornbeam allees divide the garden at Hardwick Hall.

Avenue- formed by successive pairs of trees or other identical shapes (pots or statues) flanking a drive, walk or pathway; gives a linear perspective and an impression of distance. See the grand avenues of lime trees at Hampton Court.

Belvedere- summerhouse on a high or lofty place, such as a hill, in a garden. You will find a medieval-style belvedere at Claremont Landscape Garden.

Bog Garden- a marshy area with plants that love wet feet and need permanently saturated soil and almost no drainage. A large boggy area at Savill Garden displays huge hostas and big old ferns.

Cascade- a small steep waterfall, especially one of a series. This area of England seems to be filled with them, three lovely examples are Chatsworth, Holker Hall and Wrest Park.

Cottage Garden- a grand and colorful mixture of hollyhocks, sunflowers, pansies and roses, fruits, vegetables and lots of herbs. The garden beds, dating back to the 14th Century, overflow paths leading to the front of small country homes and are often duplicated as herbaceous borders in large estates and in suburban homes. Many of Gertrude Jekyll's ideas for borders were influenced by the cottage themes.

Dovecote- a small building, raised above the ground, in which pigeons nest. See how many of these charming little buildings you can find.

Espalier- a tree or row of trees (usually fruit) trained to grow flat on a latticework or trellis. Visit the walled garden at Beningbrough Hall and see the espalied pears covering a pergola.

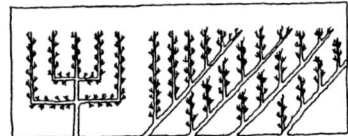

Folly- a building, often in the shape of a ruin, set in a garden or landscape purely for fun. See the many lovely follies at Studley Royal.

Grotto- a hidden underground passage, an ornamental cave; usually containing a water feature. Remember to look for the dark, mysterious grotto at Swiss Garden.

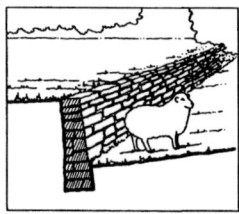

Ha-Ha- a nearly invisible sunken barrier shaped like a ditch or dry moat, used instead of a raised barrier, wall or hedge to keep cattle out of the garden. It gives the illusion the garden and the surrounding countryside are one.

Herbaceous Border- beds of hardy perennials, many grown for cut flowers, originally planted to bloom for a short time in the summer but the new "mixed" border blooms from early spring until late fall; roses and peonies are often included. You will find these in every garden, after all it wouldn't be England without it, but some of the best are at Coton Manor and the incredible borders at Newby Hall.

Knots- a pattern of intersecting bands of different herbs or low hedged planting beds; there are many examples in these tours, but one of the nicest is the sunken garden at Hatfield House.

Loggia- an arched or roofed gallery projecting from the side of a building. Look for a wonderful fountain in the loggia at Hever Castle.

Maze- a layout in which hedges are used to mark out a confusing pattern; the best known maze in England, planted in 1690, is in Hampton Court.

Obelisks- a tall, slender four sided pillar, gradually tapering as it rises, having the top in the form of a pyramid. One of these unusual monuments is featured at Studley Royal.

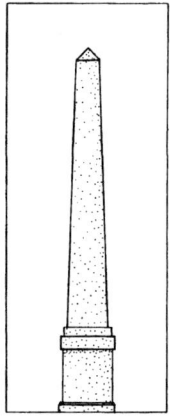

Orangery- orange trees were prized by English gardeners above almost any fruit and the orangery (or conservatory or greenhouse) was built to protect them and other tender plants from the winter cold. Two of the most famous are the Conservative Wall at Chatsworth and the Palm House at Kew.

Parterre- the ornamental garden close to the palace or house, composed of low patterns in boxwood, grass or flowers; it was invented in the 16th century for the Queen of France. There are parterres in many gardens but two of the most fabulous are the Italian Renaissance garden at Cliveden and the Victorian parterre at Harewood House.

Pele Tower- strongly built tower used for a place of refuge and look-out. Pele Towers are especially common in the northern counties of England and most were built in the 16th and 17th centuries. Pele is cognate with 'pale' which means enclosure.

Pergola- a series of constructed arches that create a pathway and can be decorative or covered with climbing and twining plants. Three different looks are the semi-circle rose pergola at St. Albans, the laburnum arch at Newby Hall and the old lime arch at Hatfield House.

Pleaching- technique used for training and shaping trees into architectural forms they would not naturally take, done by bending and intertwining branches.

Potager- the vegetable or kitchen garden. There are certainly many examples, at Holdenby House the fruits and veggies are mixed with colorful roses.

Rondel- circular grassy areas surrounded by a hedge (Kentish people used term, an area used to dry hops). As you might imagine, a fabulous beech rondel is waiting for you at Levens Hall.

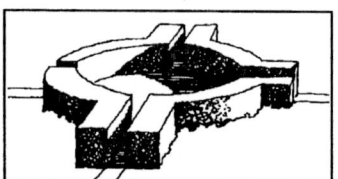

Topiary- clipped evergreens, some in elaborate forms, some in simple cones or pyramids. They came into their own in the 17th Century and were the first to go in the landscape movement. Wonderful shapes and sizes can be found in many gardens but Topiary Town is at Levens Hall.

Vista- artificially created view of the countryside usually created by planting an avenue of trees.

Garden Tours of England

GARDEN PARTICULARS

	GARDEN NAME	CITY	PHONE NUMBER	NATIONAL TRUST	MONTHS OPEN	DAYS OPEN	HOURS OPEN	FEE/ AMOUNT	FOOD SERVICE	PICNIC AREA	REST ROOM	GIFT SHOP
1	Acorn Bank Garden	Penrith, Cumbria	017683 61893	Yes	Apr thru Oct	Daily	10:00-5:30	£2.20,chd£1.10	Yes	Yes	Yes	Yes
2	Ascott	Wing, Buckingham	01296 688242	Yes	May thru Aug	Wed,last Sun	2:00-6:00	£5.00				
3	Beningbrough Hall	Shipton,Yorkshire	01904 470666	Yes	Apr thru Oct	Sat-Wed,Fri in Jul & Aug	11:00-5:00	£5.00,chd£2.50	Yes	Yes	Yes	Yes
4	Brantwood	Coniston,Cumbria	015394 41396	No	midMar-midNov	Daily	11:00-5:30	£3.90,chd£1.00	Yes	No	Yes	Yes
5	Calke Abbey	Ticknall, Derby	01332 863822	Yes	Apr thru Oct	Sat-Wed, Bk Hol Mon	11:00-5:30	£4.70,chd£2.30	Yes	Yes	Yes	Yes
6	Canons Ashby House	Daventry, Northsh	01327 860044	Yes	Apr thru Oct	Sat-Wed, Bk Hol Mon	1:00-5:30	£3.60,chd£1.80	Yes	No	Yes	Yes
7	Capel Manor	Enfield,Middlesex	01813 664442	No	Mar-Oct	Daily	10:00-5:30	£4.00,chd£2.00	Yes	No	Yes	Yes
8	Castle Ashby	Northampton, Northsh	01604 696696	No	All	Daily	10:00-5:00	£2.50,chd£1.00	Yes	Yes	Yes	Yes
9	Chatsworth	Bakewell,Derbyshire	01246 582204	No	Apr thru Oct	Daily	11:00-6:00	£3.60,chd£1.75	Yes	Yes	Yes	No
10	Chelsea Physic Garden	London		No	midApr-midOct	Wed,Sun	2:00-5:00		Yes	No	Yes	Yes
11	Claremont Landscape Garden	Esher, Surrey	(0372) 469421	Yes	Apr thru Oct	Mon-Fri Sat,Sun,Bk Hol Mon	10:00-6:00 10:00-7:00	£3.00	Yes	No	Yes	Yes
12	Cliveden	Taplow, Buck.	0628 605069	Yes	Mar thru Dec	Daily	11:00-6:30		Yes	No	Yes	Yes
13	Clumber Park	Worksop,Nottingham	01909 476592	Yes	All	Daily	10:00-6:00	£3.00	Yes	Yes	Yes	Yes
14	Colon Manor Garden	Guilsborough, Northsh	01604 740219	No	midApr thru Sep	Wed-Sun,Bk Hol Mon	12:00-5:300	£3.00,chd£1.00	Yes	No	Yes	Yes
15	Cottesbrooke Hall	Cottesbrooke,Northamp	01604 505808	No	Apr thru Sept	Tue thru Fri,Bank Hol Mon	2:00-5:30	£4.00,chd£2.00	Yes	No	Yes	Yes
16	Dalemain	Penrith,Cumbria	01768 486450	No	Apr thru Sep	Daily ex Fri & Sat	10:30-5:00	£3.00,chd free	Yes	No	Yes	Yes
17	Dorney Court	Windsor, Berkshire	01628 604638	No	July & Aug	Mon-Thurs	1:00-4:30	£4.00,chd£2.00			Yes	Yes
18	Dove Cottage	Grasmere,Cumbria	015394 35544	No	Feb-Dec	Daily	9:30-5:30		Yes	No	Yes	Yes
19	Englefield House	Reading, Berkshire	01734 302221	No	All Apr thru Jul	Mon Mon-Thur	10:00-dsk 10:00-6:00	£2.00	No	No	No	Yes
20	Fenton House	London	1071 435 3471	Yes	Apr thru Oct	Sat,Sun,Bk Hol Mon Wed-Fri	11:00-5:30 2:00-5:30	£3.60,chd£1.80				

THE MONTHS, DAYS AND TIMES OF OPERATION WERE CONFIRMED PRIOR TO PUBLICATION OF THIS BOOK. THE AUTHOR IS NOT RESPONSIBLE IF CHANGES ARE MADE TO THESE SCHEDULES. IT IS ADVISABLE TO CONFIRM THE SCHEDULE PRIOR TO SETTING OUT ON YOUR DAYS TOUR.

GARDEN PARTICULARS

	GARDEN NAME	CITY	PHONE NUMBER	NATIONAL TRUST	MONTHS OPEN	DAYS OPEN	HOURS OPEN	FEE/ AMOUNT	FOOD SERVICE	PICNIC AREA	REST ROOM	GIFT SHOP
21	Gardens of the Rose, The	St. Albans, Hert.	01727 850461	No	All	Daily	9:00-5:00	£4.00,chd free	Yes	Yes	Yes	Yes
22	Haddon Hall	Bakewell,Derbyshire	01629 812855	No	Apr thru Sep	Daily	11:00-5:45	£4.50,chd£2.80	Yes	No	Yes	Yes
23	Hampton Court	East Molesey, Surrey	0181 781 9500	No	Apr-Oct	Daily	9:30-6:00	£8.00,chd£4.90	Yes	Yes	Yes	Yes
24	Harewood House	Leeds, West Yorkshire	0113 288 6331	No	midMar thru Oct	Daily	10:00-6:00	£5.50,chd£3.00	Yes	Yes	Yes	Yes
25	Hardwick Hall	Chesterfield,Derby	01246 850430	Yes	Apr thru Oct	Daily	12:00-6:30	£2.50,chd£1.00	Yes	No	Yes	Yes
26	Harlow Carr Botanic Garden	Harrogate,Yorkshire	01423 565418	No	All	Daily	9:30-6:00	£3.30,chd free	Yes	Yes	Yes	Yes
27	Hatfield House	Hatfield, Hertfordshire	01707 262823	No	Apr thru Sep	Daily	11:00-6:00	£5.20,chd£3.30	Yes	Yes	Yes	Yes
28	Holdenby House	Holdenby, Nortish	01604 770074	No	midApr thru Sep	Daily exSat	2:00-6:00	£3.00,chd£2.00	Yes	No	Yes	Yes
29	Holehird	Windermere, Cumbria	01539 446008	No	All	Daily	9:00-6:00	£1.00	No	No	No	Yes
30	Holker Hall	Grange-over-Sands,Cum	015395 58328	No	Apr thru Oct	Daily ex Sat	10:00-6:00	£3.35,chd£1.90	Yes	No	Yes	Yes
31	Hughenden Manor	High Wycombe, Buck.	01494 532580	Yes	Apr thru Oct	Wed-Sun,Bk Hol Mon	1:00-5:00	£3.70,chd£1.85	Yes	Yes	Yes	Yes
32	Hutton-in-the-Forest	Penrith,Cumbria	01768 484449	No	May thru Sep	Daily ex Sat	11:00-5:00	£2.50,chd free	Yes	Yes	Yes	Yes
33	Kedleston Hall	Derby, Derbyshire	01332 842191	Yes	Apr thru Oct	Sat-Wed	11:00-5:30	£2.00,chd£1.00	Yes	No	Yes	Yes
34	Kensington Gardens	London	0171 376 2452	No	All	Daily	9:00-dusk	None	No	Yes	Yes	No
35	Kew, Royal Botanic Garden	Kew, Surrey	0181 940 1171	No	All	Daily	9:30-6:00	£4.50,chd£2.50	Yes	No	Yes	Yes
36	Knebworth House	Knebworth,Hert.	01438 812661	No	lateMay-Sept	Daily	11:00-5:30	£4.00	Yes	Yes	Yes	Yes
37	Leighton Hall	Carnforth,Lancashire	01524 734474	No	May -Sept	Daily	2:00-5:00	£3.60,chd£2.40	Yes	Yes	Yes	Yes
38	Levens Hall	Kendal, Cumbria	01539 560321	No	Apr thru midOct	Sun-Thur	11:00-5:00	£3.50,chd£1.80	Yes	No	Yes	Yes
39	Lingholm Gardens	CLOSED										
40	Lotherton Hall	Garforth,West York	0113 2813723	No	All	Daily	10:30-6:00		Yes	Yes	Yes	Yes
41	Luton Hoo	CLOSED PERMANENTLY										
42	Melbourne Hall	Melbourne,Derbyshire	01332 862502	No	Apr thru Sep	Wed,Sat,Sun, bk hol Mon	2:00-6:00	£3.00,chd£2.00	Yes	No	Yes	Yes
43	Muncaster Castle	Ravenglass, Cumbria	01229 717614	No	Apr thru Oct	Daily	11:00-5:00	£3.50,chd£2.00	Yes	No	Yes	Yes

THE MONTHS, DAYS AND TIMES OF OPERATION WERE CONFIRMED PRIOR TO PUBLICATION OF THIS BOOK. THE AUTHOR IS NOT RESPONSIBLE IF CHANGES ARE MADE TO THESE SCHEDULES. IT IS ADVISABLE TO CONFIRM THE SCHEDULE PRIOR TO SETTING OUT ON YOUR DAY'S TOUR.

Garden Tours of England

GARDEN PARTICULARS

	GARDEN NAME	CITY	PHONE NUMBER	NATIONAL TRUST	MONTHS OPEN	DAYS OPEN	HOURS OPEN	FEE/ AMOUNT	FOOD SERVICE	PICNIC AREA	REST ROOM	GIFT SHOP
44	Myddelton House Gardens	Enfield, Middlesex	01992 717711	No	Feb-Oct	Mon-Fri	10:00-3:30	£1.80	No	No	Yes	Yes
45	Newby Hall	Ripon, Yorkshire	01423 322583	No	Apr thru Sep	Daily ex Mon	11:00-5:30	£5.40,chd£3.20	Yes	Yes	Yes	Yes
46	Newstead Abbey	Newstead, Nottingham	01623 793557	No	Apr thru Sep	Daily	9:00-6:00	£3.50,chd£1.00	Yes	No	Yes	Yes
47	Parcevall Hall Gardens	Skipton, Yorkshire	01756 720311	No	Apr thru Oct	Daily	10:00-6:00	£2.00	Yes	Yes	Yes	Yes
48	Renishaw Hall	Sheffield, Derbyshire	01777 860755	No	Apr to midSep	Fri,Sat,Sun,Bk Hol Mon	10:30-4:30	£3.00,chd£1.00	Yes	No	Yes	No
49	Rydal Mount	Ambleside, Cumbria	01539 433002	No	Mar-Oct	Daily	9:30-5:00	£3.00,chd£1.00	No	No	No	No
50	The Savill Garden/Valley Garden	Windsor Great Pk,Berk	01753 860222	No	Mar-Oct	Daily	10:00-6:00	£3.50,chd-free	Yes	No	Yes	Yes
51	Sizergh Castle	Kendal, Cumbria	01539 560070	Yes	Apr thru Oct	Sun-Thurs	12:30-5:30	£2.00,chd£1.00	Yes	Yes	Yes	Yes
52	Stowe Landscape Garden	Buckingham, Buck.	01280 822850	Yes	midApr-5Jul 7Jul-8Sep	Mon,Wed,Fri,Sun Daily	10:00-5:00	£4.00	Yes	Yes	Yes	Yes
53	Studley Royal/Fountains Abbey	Ripon, Yorkshire	01765 608888	Yes	Apr thru Sep	Daily	10:00-7:00	£4.00,chd£2.00	Yes	No	Yes	Yes
54	Sulgrave Manor	Sulgrave, Northsh	01295 760205	No	Apr thru Oct	Daily except Wed	2:00-5:30	£3.50,chd£1.75	Yes	No	Yes	Yes
55	Swiss Garden	Old Warden, Bed.	01767 627666	No	Mar-Sep	Sat,Sun,Bk Hol	10:00-6:00	£2.50	Yes	Yes	Yes	No
56	Wisely Garden	Woking, Surry	01483 224234	No	All	Daily	10:00-7:00	£4.90,chd£1.75	Yes	Yes	Yes	Yes
57	Wrest Park & Gardens	Silsoe, Bedfordshire	01525 860152	No	Apr thru Sep	Sat,Sun,Bk Hol Mon	10:00-6:00	£2.50,chd£1.30	Yes	Yes	Yes	No

THE MONTHS, DAYS AND TIMES OF OPERATION WERE CONFIRMED PRIOR TO PUBLICATION OF THIS BOOK. THE AUTHOR IS NOT RESPONSIBLE IF CHANGES ARE MADE TO THESE SCHEDULES. IT IS ADVISABLE TO CONFIRM THE SCHEDULE PRIOR TO SETTING OUT ON YOUR DAY'S TOUR.

• LIST OF PUBLICATIONS •

Garden Books

"Yellow Book", Gardens of England and Wales, for a copy send $18.00 to: The National Gardens Scheme, Hatchlands Park, East Clandon, Guildford, Surrey, GU4 7RT

Garden Style by Penelope Hobhouse; Little, Brown & Company, 1988

A Book of Gardening- The National Trust by Penelope Hobhouse; Little, Brown & Company, 1986

Flower Gardens by Penelope Hobhouse, Little, Brown & Co., 1991

The Ordnance Survey Guide to Gardens in England; W.W. Norton & Company, 1986

The Country House Garden by Gervase Jackson-Stops; Pavilion Books Limited, 1987

The Garden Makers by George Plumptre; Random House, 1993

One Hundred English Gardens by Patrick Taylor; Rizzoli International Publications, Inc, 1996

The National Trust Gardens Handbook, for a copy contact: The National Trust, 36 Queen Anne's Gate, London SW1H 9AS or phone 0171 222 9251

Gardens of the National Trust by Graham Thomas, The National Trust/Weidenfeld & Nicolson, London, 1979

Gardens of England, Scotland & Wales By Hazel Evens, George Philip Limited, 1991

The History of Gardens by Christopher Thacker, University of California Press, 1979

The Art of Planting by Rosemary Verey; Little, Brown & Co., 1990

The Gardens of England, The Counties of Kent, Surrey and Sussex by Rob Talbot & Robin Whiteman; Weidenfeld and Nicolson, London, 1995

The Formal Garden by Mark Laird; Thames and Hudson, London, 1992

Hudson's Historic Houses & Gardens, Norman Hudson & Co., Banbury; bookstore or 01295 750750

Garden Magazine

The English Garden, Romsey Publishing Co., London subscription enquires: 1-800-998-0807

Hotels and B & B's

Bed and Breakfast for Garden Lovers, for a copy send a self addressed envelope with 3 international reply-paid coupons to: BBGL, Handywater Farm, Sibford Gower, Banbury, Oxfordshire OX15 5AE

Cotswold Retreats, for a copy call: Paula at 01608 737222 or Sue at 01608 684310 or fax 01608 684310

The National Trust Bed and Breakfast, for a copy contact: The National Trust, 36 Queen Anne's Gate, London SW1H 9AS or phone 0171 222 9251

England, Charming Bed & Breakfasts; Karen Brown; Travel Press, 1996 or phone (415) 342-9117

England, Wales & Scotland, Charming Hotels & Itineraries; Karen Brown; Travel Press, 1996 or phone (415) 342-9117

Johansens Recommended Hotels, Great Britain & Ireland and
Johansens Recommended Country Houses & Small Hotels
Johansens, London; bookstores or phone 0171 490 3090

Index

A

ACORN BANK GARDEN 63, 89
Aislabie, John 71, 101
Allee 121
Ambleside 11, 12, 67
American flag 39
ARTS & CRAFTS MOVEMENT 107, 116
ASCOTT 89
Ascott Park 15
Astor, William Waldorf 25
Austin, David 60
Avenue 121

B

Bakewell, Robert 43
Balmoral Hotel 5
Banks, Joseph 85, 101
Barnsley House 73, 80, 111
Barry, Charles 25, 76, 102, 116
Battle of Waterloo 49, 53
Beaumont, Guillaume 60, 102
Bedfordshire 15
Belvedere 121
BENINGBROUGH HALL 79, 81, 89
Bog Garden 121
Bowles, E.A. 29, 102
Bowness 11, 12
BRANTWOOD 67, 89
Bray-on-Thames 5
Bridgeman, Charles 19, 20, 25, 40, 103, 114
British Museum 83
Brown, 'Capability' 19, 20, 33, 40, 48, 56, 76, 103
Bruce, Ken 6

C

CALKE ABBEY 89
Canadian Air Force 81
CANONS ASHBY HOUSE 39, 41, 90
CAPEL MANOR 90
Cascade 48, 56, 61
CASTLE ASHBY 35, 90, 103
Charles I 37
Charles II 20
CHATSWORTH 47, 48, 55, 56, 90, 103, 108
CHELSEA PHYSIC GARDEN 83, 90
Chippendale, Thomas 76
Chunnel 7
Church, Thomas 118
Churchill, Winston 27
CLAREMONT LANDSCAPE GARDEN 19, 51, 91, 103, 106, 110
CLIVEDEN 5, 23, 25, 91, 102
CLUMBER PARK 91, 104
Coniston 12
Coniston Water 11, 12
COTON MANOR GARDEN 35, 36, 91
Cottage Garden 121
COTTESBROOKE HALL 91
Czar Nicholas 48, 56

D

DALEMAIN 63, 64, 92
Derbyshire 13
Dickens, Charles 27
Domesday 47, 57
DORNEY COURT 92
DOVE COTTAGE
    12, 67, 68, 92
Dovecote 121
Duchene, Achille 117

E

EARLY 20th CENTURY 117
Elizabeth I 28, 35, 37
ENGLEFIELD HOUSE 23, 92
Eric Savill 24
Espalier 121
Eton College 15
Eurostar 7

F

FENTON HOUSE 83, 92
Folly 121
Forest of Inglewood 65
FORMAL GARDEN DESIGN
    113
Forsyth, William 83
FOUNTAINS ABBEY 71, 99

G

GARDENS OF THE ROSE
    29, 31, 93
George II 20, 84
George III 20, 85
George VI 24
Gilpin, William Sawrey 104
Glossop 13
golf 49, 53
Gondola 12, 67

Grange-over-Sands 5
Grange-upon-Sands 13
Grasmere 67
Graythwaite Manor 5, 13
Grotto 122

H

Ha-Ha 122
HADDON HALL 47, 55, 57, 93
HAMPTON COURT
    19, 20, 93, 106
HARDWICK HALL 51, 55, 93
HAREWOOD HOUSE
    75, 76, 94, 102, 103, 109
Harewood Lake 76
HARLOW CARR BOTANICAL
    GARDENS 75, 79, 94
Harrogate 5, 15, 75
HATFIELD HOUSE
    27, 28, 94, 110
Hatton, Christopher 37
Henry VIII 35
Herbaceous Border 122
Hidcote Manor 73, 80, 105
Hill Top 12
Himalayon Poppies 64
Hobhouse, Penelope 119
HOLDENBY HOUSE 35, 37, 94
HOLEHIRD 67, 69, 94
HOLKER HALL 59, 61, 95
Howard, Ebenezer 15
HUGHENDEN MANOR 95
HUTTON-IN-THE-FOREST
    63, 65, 95

J

Jekyll, Gertrude
    25, 27, 44, 49, 53, 105, 118
Jellicoe, Geoffrey 21, 25, 119
Johnston, Lawrence
    73, 80, 105, 118

K

KEDLESTON HALL
  43, 44, 95, 105
KENSINGTON GARDENS
  84, 95
Kensington Palace 83, 84
Kent, William
  19, 20, 40, 106, 114
KEW, ROYAL BOTANICAL
  GARDEN 83, 101
KEW, ROYAL BOTANICAL
  GARDENS 85, 96
KNEBWORTH HOUSE
  27, 96, 105
Knots 122

L

Lake District
  11, 15, 59, 63, 67, 69, 71, 108
Lake Windermere 11
"LANDSCAPE MOVEMENT"
  114
Langdale Chase Hotel 5
LATE 20th CENTURY 119
LEIGHTON HALL 96
Letchworth 15
LEVENS HALL 59, 60, 96, 102
Lloyd, Christopher 117, 119
Loggia 122
London 7, 15, 83, 84
London, George
  48, 56, 106, 114
London, Henry 41
Lord Byron 45, 52
LOTHERTON HALL 75, 77, 97
Lutyens, Edwin
  27, 44, 49, 53, 107, 118

M

Maidenhead 5

Matlock 5, 13
Maze 122
McCartney, Paul 8
MELBOURNE HALL
  43, 97, 106
MID 20th CENTUR 118
Minster 14
Monkey Island Hotel 5
Morris, William 107, 117
MUNCASTER CASTLE 97
Museum of Garden History 15
MYDDELTON HOUSE GAR-
  DEN 27, 102
MYDDELTON HOUSE GAR-
  DENS 29, 97

N

National Portrait Gallery 81
National Trust
  6, 8, 12, 19, 25, 40, 41, 44,
  51, 55, 59, 81, 108
New Bath Hotel 5
NEWBY HALL
  71, 73, 79, 80, 97
NEWSTEAD ABBEY
  43, 45, 51, 52, 98
Northern Horticultural Society
  75, 79
Nottingham Castle 15

O

Oast House 123
Obelisks 123
Orangery 123

P

Palladio 43, 44
PARCEVALL HALL GARDEN
  71, 72, 98

133

Paris 7
Parterre 123
Paxton, Joseph
    48, 56, 61, 108, 116
PEAK DISTRICT 13
Peak National Park 13
Pele Tower 59, 60, 65
Penrith 63
Pergola 123
Peter Rabbit 12
Peto, Harold 117, 118
Pleaching 124
Potager 124
Potter, Beatrix 12, 108
Prestbury 14
Princess Ausgusta 85

Q

Queen Victoria 20, 28

R

Ransome, Arthur 12
Redcoats Farmhouse Hotel 5
RENISHAW HALL 49
RENISHAW HALL
    47, 51, 53, 98
Repton, Humphry
    76, 109, 115, 116
River Ure 73
River Wye 47, 57
Robinson, William 117
Rondel 124
Royal National Rose Society
    29, 31
Royal Oak Foundation 8
Ruskin, John 12, 67, 109
RYDAL MOUNT 12, 67, 68, 98

S

Sackville-West, Vita 118

SAVILL GARDEN 23, 24, 99
Sherwood Forest 15
Shuttleworth Collection 15
Shuttleworth, Joseph 32
Sitwell, George 49, 53
SIZERGH CASTLE 59, 99
Society of Apothecaries 83
St. Albans 27
St. Albans 29, 31
Steamboat Museum 12
STOWE LANDSCAPE GARDEN
    40, 99, 103, 106, 111
STUDLEY ROYAL 71, 99, 101
Sulgrave 15
SULGRAVE MANOR
    15, 39, 100
SWISS GARDEN
    15, 31, 32, 100

T

Thomas, Graham Stuart 110
Topiary 124
Topiary Town 60
Tower of London 83
Tradescant, John, the Elder
    28, 110
Transportation 7

U

U.C. Berkeley 27

V

Valley Garden 23, 24
Van Nost, John 43
Vanbrugh, John 19, 111, 114
Verey, Rosemary 37, 111, 119
Victorian Palm House 85
VICTORIAN PERIOD 115
Vista 124

W

Walpole, Hugh 12
War of the Roses 29
Washington, George 39, 115
William & Mary 20
Willmott, Ellen 73, 80, 111
Wilson, E.H. 72
Wilson, G.F. 21
Wimbledon 15
Winderemere 5
Windermere 7, 11, 12
Windermere Lake 12
Windsor Castle 15
Windsor Great Park 24
Wise, George 41
Wise, Henry 43, 48, 56, 114
WISLEY GARDEN
    19, 21, 51, 100
Wordsworth, William 12, 67, 68
Wren, Christopher 20, 84
WREST PARK 31, 33, 100, 103
Wright, Frank Lloyd 118

Y

Yellow Book 5
York 7, 14, 71

• ORDER FORM •

- Fax Orders: (925) 934-7761 (send this form)
- On-Line orders: Bonnie Randall-- ukgarden@lanminds.com
- Postal Orders: Windsor Hill Publishing,
  119 Poppy Court, Walnut Creek, Ca. 94596, U.S.A.
- Telephone orders: (925) 934-7761

Please send ____ copies of Garden Tours of England -The Cotswolds

and/or ____ copies of Garden Tours of England-The Southern Region

and/or ____ copies of Garden Tours of England- London to The Lake District

Price $14.95 per copy

Sales tax for those books shipped in California is 8.25%.

Shipping: Book rate is $2.00 for the first book and 75 cents for each additional book (shipping may take 3 to 4 weeks). Air Mail is $3.50 per book.

Please Print:

Name:_____

Address:_____

City:_____State_____Zip:_____

Telephone:_____

		Total
Tour Books	____x $14.95	
Tax	8.25% in Calif.	
Shipping		
Total		

Payment:
☐ Check

▫ Credit Card: ▫ VISA, ▫ MasterCard

Card number:_____Exp Date:_____

Name on card:_____

Signature:_____

• ORDER FORM •

- Fax Orders: (925) 934-7761 (send this form)
- On-Line orders: Bonnie Randall-- ukgarden@lanminds.com
- Postal Orders: Windsor Hill Publishing,
  119 Poppy Court, Walnut Creek, Ca. 94596, U.S.A.
- Telephone orders: (925) 934-7761

Please send ____ copies of Garden Tours of England -The Cotswolds

and/or ____ copies of Garden Tours of England-The Southern Region

and/or ____ copies of Garden Tours of England- London to The Lake District

Price $14.95 per copy

Sales tax for those books shipped in California is 8.25%.
Shipping: Book rate is $2.00 for the first book and 75 cents for each additional book (shipping may take 3 to 4 weeks). Air Mail is $3.50 per book.

Please Print:

Name:_____

Address:_____

City:_____State_____Zip:_____

Telephone:_____

		Total
Tour Books	____x $14.95	
Tax	8.25% in Calif.	
Shipping		
Total		

Payment:
▫ Check

▫ Credit Card: ▫ VISA, ▫ MasterCard

Card number:_____Exp Date:_____

Name on card:_____

Signature:_____